SKYSCRAPERS
AND OTHER ESSAYS

MACMILLAN AND CO., Limited
LONDON · BOMBAY · CALCUTTA · MADRAS
MELBOURNE

THE MACMILLAN COMPANY
NEW YORK · BOSTON · CHICAGO
DALLAS · ATLANTA · SAN FRANCISCO

THE MACMILLAN COMPANY
OF CANADA, LIMITED
TORONTO

SKYSCRAPERS
AND OTHER ESSAYS

BY
L. B. NAMIER

MACMILLAN AND CO., LIMITED
ST. MARTIN'S STREET, LONDON
1931

COPYRIGHT

PRINTED IN GREAT BRITAIN

INTRODUCTION

For the last eighteen years I have been writing for the Press, mostly for weekly papers. The sum-total of my contributions in that length of time would probably be much too small to qualify me for a journalist; and time defeats me once more in the matter of summarising my current literary work in book form. Essays which might stand the test of reproduction after a year or two will not stand it after ten or fifteen years. Here I have picked out twenty essays which, I think, do stand that test; and in reproducing them I have made no attempt at " modernising " them. Except for some small changes such as every writer will make on going once more through his work, they appear in their original form ; the reader should therefore each time note the date at which the essay was first published. One essay, if compared with its original text, would appear to have been expanded; the truth is that, when first published, it had been cut down to suit the requirements of the paper, and has now been restored to its full length.

My best thanks are due to the editors and owners of the various papers in which these essays were originally published for giving me permission to republish them.

L. B. NAMIER.

15, *Gloucester Walk,*
London, W.8.
January 26th, 1931.

CONTENTS

	PAGE
SKYSCRAPERS	1
THE HYPHENATED	9
THE DISINHERITANCE OF AMERICA	21
PUBLIC OPINION AND REPRESENTATIVE GOVERNMENT	34
THE BIOGRAPHY OF ORDINARY MEN	44
COMMUNITIES	54
THE EUROPEAN SITUATION	62
GERMANS AND RUSSIA	73
TROTSKY	81
METTERNICH'S DOCTRINE	95
THE AUSTRIAN REVOLUTION	103
PRESIDENT MASARYK	113
THE VICTORY OF AN IDEA	122
ZIONISM	128
THEODOR HERZL	138
AGRARIAN REVOLUTION	145
THE PEASANT AND THE STATE	156
CURRENCIES AND EXCHANGES IN AN EAST GALICIAN VILLAGE	163
LORD FIFE AND HIS FACTOR	173
FAMILY HISTORY	181

SKYSCRAPERS
AND OTHER ESSAYS

SKYSCRAPERS

(" *The Nation and Athenæum*," September 10th, 1927)

THE Statue of Liberty was raised on Bedloe Island to deliver America's first message to those who approach her shore. Large and crude, it is a symbol of French philosophy misplaced on Anglo-Saxon soil; it suited the exuberance and conceit of the American as formed by the Revolution. The doctrine it proclaims many have by now come to doubt, while for others, the new-comers, it has no real meaning; the statue remains mute to the stranger. But when in the early morning the weary ocean boat glides up the Hudson River, a mirage arises before his eyes, incongruous at first, wondrous when found to be real. He sees the long-drawn, even line of Manhattan Island with the rows of ordinary houses, but high above the grey gloom and the mist of the river-side arise gigantic structures, a new world in different dimensions. The dim houses along the river recede, like an uncertain reminiscence, and the eye fastens on the city above the clouds, which in its splendid whiteness reflects the morning sun. The skyscrapers, superhuman, seemingly conscious of their own mystic symbolism, deliver America's message of a colossal reality, of a new life and its unbridled force.

Architecture works direct, like music, and is social in character as no other art. Painting and poetry have to picture objects and to relate events, even when they aim at reproducing moods or emotions. Various forms of "expressionism" represent desperate and fundamentally hopeless attempts to conquer for them the unmaterial independence of music. There is nothing to be depicted or related in architecture; social needs are its occasions; it starts by supplying the framework for mass activities, and becomes art when, in a mute, subconscious way, it expresses their nature. Small private houses are no proper objects for it; the Greeks wisely refrained from attempting it on them; in mediæval Oxford architecture was applied to colleges, not to lodging-houses. But an age which, preoccupied with the individual, well-nigh forgot the community, built pillars only fit to bear the number of the house, reproduced prettiness in endless rows of six-roomed brick houses, and when it tried to impart originality to units in a crowd, produced garden suburbs, where houses seem to make faces at each other to escape looking alike. The true architecture of ordinary houses is along the line of social agglomeration, in the joint character of the street. Its profile, the curve of a crescent, the grouping of avenues, constitute a horizontal type of architecture, and express the partial symbiosis of a town population co-operating within an individualist system.

The life of communities is recorded in their monumental structures. The Chinese Wall, built for eminently practical purposes, was none the less a spiritual symbol. The Pyramids speak of the dominion of the Pharaohs over a people confined by the desert, not joined by a social purpose, a mass as primitive in shape as are those blind mountain-monuments of aimless toil.[1] In the Middle Ages men united in Church and State, for prayer and defence, and built cathedrals and fortresses : cathedrals too vast for their congregations, intended for Him in whose name they gathered, originating in a social need, and rising to the level of an idea ; and fortresses, rocks upon rocks, ruthless and defiant, grim as the armour of ancient Samurais, meant to strike terror. The distinguishing peculiarity of our

---

[1] Not all historical generalisations in this particular essay should be taken as considered professional judgments.

own age is its gigantic social and economic organisation of human labour for purposes of everyday life; the skyscrapers are its architectural expression.

The first skyscrapers arose in America, where economic forces and factors exercise a more absolute sway than in any other country. Sometimes an attempt is made to explain their origin by the peculiar conditions of Manhattan Island, its narrow shape, the high price of building ground, its live rock which offers a suitable foundation for enormous structures, etc. One might as well explain Gothic spires by the narrow compass of mediæval towns—but high steeples and low chapels so faithfully reproduce the contrast between the hierarchical organisation of traditional, catholic churches and the inward, individualised religion of independent congregations, that with us the creeds have come to be described in terms of architecture. Nor is the economy of skyscrapers incontestably proved; or buildings of a different type would not arise alongside of them. Nearer the mark is perhaps the attempt to explain them by the American passion for " records," the secret satisfaction of the American even at disasters or heat waves in his country exceeding anything known elsewhere. Cuvier maintained that every continent has certain features which it tends to reproduce in all it bears.

SKYSCRAPERS

America's dominant feature, in land, rivers and waterfalls, trees and men, is their colossal size and their comparative uniformity; they are fit material for records and statistics. The skyscrapers, in their origin, are no doubt connected with the American predilection for high figures; and yet in their development they mark a gradual transition from aggregation to integration, from masses to mass individuality, from sheer numbers to inner unity.

During the period of rapid expansion, America's social life became amorphous. A human flood spread with increasing rapidity over an empty continent, unbound and uniform; in its socially unstratified, historically uneventful existence numbers were the one striking, dominant factor. " The ratio of population is now a fundamental subject," wrote, in 1767, Ezra Stiles (subsequently President of Yale College), who, though still mildly interested in the sea-serpent and the King of Prussia, eagerly compiled statistics, the biography of the masses. The earliest skyscrapers corresponded to the stage in America's development when comparatively primitive forms were reproduced on a numerically unprecedented scale. They were ordinary houses enormously magnified, infinite collections of windows in gigantic frameworks, symbols of multiplicity rather than of organisation; their unity was in juxtaposition, but there was no shape in them. Still, a vast growth in numbers almost invariably ends by producing a difference in kind; for masses tend to develop a peculiar individuality of their own. A gigantic office building is something fundamentally different from a house, and trades unions and trusts cannot be made to conform to the social structure of Cobdenite individualism. Modern social and economic life gradually creates its own specific style and law, and in their morphology will be its soul; but their forms take a long time to develop, and cannot be foretold or anticipated; and as they assert themselves, they are bound to provoke the ire and passionate resistance of those who, socially and economically, are "the dead above ground." Like the grin of the Cheshire cat, the past hovers over mankind.

When the builders first came to realise the possibilities of shape in skyscrapers, they turned for it to the past—even the boldest flights of imagination are on wings made, like those of Icarus, of borrowed plumes; skyscrapers were given the outlines of cathedrals or of palatial fortresses. But the life of the new mass individuality was bound to break through inherited forms. There had to be windows, innumerable windows, which, when aglow at night, speak of labour and economic purpose, such as was not where men gathered for prayer and defence; the pattern of light which skyscrapers weave in the darkness is one test for their architecture. Moreover, the very shape of the skyscrapers barred close imitation. The basic design of Western churches is that of a quadruped, the tower, in front, being raised like a head above the long line of the body. But the skyscrapers are the bipeds of architectural creation—they are vertical streets that have risen to their feet and stand upright like human beings. There is a beauty of proportion in them other than in creatures riveted to the ground. Subconsciously the skyscraper of about 1910 is related to the human form. The New York Municipal Building is fine; it is like a man with broad shoulders; his head is bent in a brooding attitude; in darkness and mist (when details are effaced and the glare of the crown is softened) it resembles Rodin's "Penseur." The Woolworth Building is hideous; it has a long neck and cramped, narrow shoulders; from the municipal garden it looks like a giraffe, the joy of children and caricaturists; from the river like a bird with its wings tied to the back; and its misshapen body is covered with petty decoration which, to say the least, is wasted, for it becomes practically invisible at the distance, from which alone a proper view is obtained of the building.

In the very nature of things, decorative detail does not suit modern mass individuality; decoration has to be individual, while single units in a crowd have no separate independent existence. The champion dressed for battle; the dress of organised masses is the " uniform "; the incidents in their life are numerical, statistical; outlines and proportions alone count in mass individuality. There is a deep, hidden efficiency in it, a subordination to practical purpose, an austerity which discards show, a greatness which appears only when its personality is viewed as a whole. For good and evil, we have in a thousand ways outgrown the day of the lonely individual; the direction of mass effort takes the place of solitary achievement. The mass-individuality becomes multiple, and a third stage is being reached in the architecture of skyscrapers—the most recent among them are no longer overgrown houses or lonely giants, but phantom cities, colossal piles, rising in " zones," with vast articulated bodies, silent Towers of Babel.

THE HYPHENATED

(" *The New Statesman,*" *March* 4*th*, 1916)

[Note the date of the essay; it has not been " modernised."]

THE only types of hyphenated citizens which practically do not exist in the United States are the English-Americans and the Scotch-Americans. Hardly anyone thinks in America of even the most recent British extraction as foreign. Not one man in a thousand would be able to say, without referring to books, how many generations ago President Wilson's British ancestors had come over to America; had he any other foreign ancestors within the last two or three generations, it would be a fact of common knowledge. Two prominent members of his Cabinet are British-born; should a serious conflict of interests or opinions occur between the United States and the British Empire, no more attention would be paid in America to their foreign origin than would recently have been given in England to the fact that one prominent member of the British Cabinet was on his mother's side of American descent. Englishmen would strongly resent it should anyone of British birth act as a representative of some other State in a way contrary to the interests of the British Empire. But the feeling would hardly show itself in relation to those who have found their new home in the States. The treaty concluded a short time ago between Great Britain and America, whereby a citizen of either State on becoming naturalised in the other automatically loses his original nationality, gives a legal expression to an actual state of affairs. But had the peculiar relation in which the two nations stand to one another been clearly recognised, and had its foundations and consequences been carefully examined, action of a very different kind might have ensued. There are hardly any other two great communities which could as easily face and accept double and common citizenship in the case of some of their members as could Great Britain and the United States. A transfer of allegiance from the one to the other is so easy that it need not necessarily be exclusive.

It is perfectly true that the man who has received his education in Great Britain will differ all his life from the man who has been brought up in America. But it is equally obvious that the mere fact that a man belongs to a type which is not " autochthonous " in the country does not necessarily interfere with his citizenship; the question is rather how his particular type and mentality fit into his new surroundings. For a German, a

Pole, or a Greek settling in America, the transition is almost violent; it implies the uprooting of certain habits and ideas, the grafting on of fresh ones. He seeks refuge and rest in hyphenation. There is a constant looking backwards. Of the high aims and ideals which had been dear to him in his old home, his fellow-citizens in the new country are totally ignorant. If he wishes to preserve his own ideals, he must remain distinct from his neighbours. If he transmits them to his children, his children will remain hybrids, they will be "hyphenated"; and all "hyphenation" forms a differential distinction, and thereby a restriction on the completeness of citizenship. If he does not transmit his original national inheritance to his children, he feels that with his death something must die which had possessed its own life and value, but must perish without achievement. There is sadness in the death of nationality. The children of the foreign immigrant will no longer understand something which they are by nature capable of making their own; they do not receive the inheritance for which they are best fitted; the labour of generations is lost, a flame has burnt in vain, a fire has died out without fostering life. Those who feel inclined to jeer at "hyphenation" or to criticise its bearers had better pause and try to understand their position. Hyphenation is, perhaps, still a fruitful way of preserving living values; at least, it is a subconscious attempt in that direction. The human soul turns to something which had formed the deepest meaning of its life, and whispers the fatal words of Faust, " Tarry a while, thou art so fair."

Hyphenation is a real tragedy; but the thing which concerns us here is that it does not work for good citizenship; it is contrary to the union with one's fellow-citizens which is the basis of " community." It hardly ever occurs in the case of the Britisher in the United States, or of the American in the British Empire. The outward forms of living in the two countries are different; still, migration implies no real break. The political forms, and hence the *formal* problems of politics, are different in the two countries. Yet at the present day we are confronted in both societies with the same questions, not merely of a social and economic nature—those are now more or less common to the whole Western world—but of a " political " character in the truest meaning of the term. The problems of centralisation and devolution, of government by representative assemblies and plebiscitarian autocracy in the person of Prime Minister or President, of direct popular government and government through organised parties, are very much alike in both countries; examples from one could be quoted in the other as leading cases, just as legal arguments are mutually quoted in the law courts of the two countries. There are certain fundamental ideas, many of which can be traced back to the Puritan Commonwealth, that supply a common denominator for the political life of all Anglo-Saxon countries. Were Englishmen once more turned loose on a vacant American Continent, they would in all probability build up a Commonwealth in all essentials very much like the one which is now known as the United States of North America. Were the same ground opened to the free civic activities of Germans, Poles, Italians or Spaniards, the result would beyond doubt be a very different one. Every man carries within himself component lines of the elaborate pattern of State or Commonwealth. The Britisher fits himself almost without readjustment into the American scheme of things, and *vice versa*.

It is, therefore, but natural if the Englishman settled in the States becomes an American without any of the reservations implied in hyphenation. Less natural is the treatment which he would receive if he dared to manifest any feeling for the country of his origin or for the home of his ancestors; his hyphenated fellow-citizens would shriek "Treason."[1] Have not Steuben,

[1] On May 9th, 1913, the American Committee for the Celebration of the one-hundredth Anniversary of Peace among the English-speaking peoples gave a dinner at the Hotel Astor at New York in honour of the delegates from England, Canada,

Lafayette and Kosciuszko (and also George Washington [1]) freed America from the yoke of Britain's cruel oppression? Have we forgotten the glorious " Fourth of July "? No, it will not

Australia and the Municipality of Ghent, who had come to discuss the forthcoming Peace Celebrations. Mr. Joseph Choate presided, Secretary Bryan and a number of foreign ambassadors were present. At that dinner Professor Muensterberg warned the Committee against giving to the Celebrations an exclusively Anglo-Saxon character, and declared that " there are many who think that the purpose of this whole movement is to bring America to the service of England in order to fight Germany."

On the same night the first annual dinner of the German Publications Society was held at the Plaza Hotel. The German Ambassador, Count Bernstorff, was present; a few delegates, including an English Member of Parliament, came from their dinner at the Hotel Astor " to express their goodwill." They thus had the opportunity of hearing the following remarks made by Herr Theodor Sutro, President of the German Publications Society :—

" At the Hotel Astor to-night, they are dining and wining the delegates from the English-speaking countries of the World. . . . They may well celebrate, seeing what little peace there was before that date between England and America, how during the War of the Revolution England had tried her best to crush the struggle of the American Colonies for independence, and how she had fomented the War of 1812 by plotting for years the disruption of the young Republic.

" . . . I cannot help thinking that it is, after all, not so superlatively to the credit of the Anglo-Saxon race that it has practically lived at peace with itself for a single century, and I cannot understand why there should be on that account such wild rejoicing, such extravagant self-laudation or such tremendous demonstration."

[1] Washington wrote to Gouverneur Morris on July 24th, 1778: " I do most devoutly wish that we had not a single foreigner amongst us, except the Marquis de Lafayette."

be forgotten as long as one single man within the Union still finds serious difficulties in talking English. The foreigner feels that the Revolution is a covenant between him and America. Were it forgotten, the English-speaking American might feel that he had a prior claim with regard to the North American Continent. The Revolutionary Legend remains a kind of promise concerning America's cosmopolitan attitude towards Europe. The Revolution ended with a renunciation of Englishry; in its final stages the help of a foreign Power and of foreign adventurers was accepted in a struggle which had originally been a domestic quarrel, an internal convulsion of the Anglo-Saxon world. The memory of these few stray foreign adventurers has been glorified. To them the foreign immigrant directs his gaze; he discovers gods of his own in the American mythology; they are a bond between him and America, they form the basis for a claim which he makes on the country. On the " Fourth of July " he rejoices over something which he considers the birthday of his America. His Anglo-Saxon teachers, many of whom have come over long after 1783, have taught him to celebrate that day; he has grasped its meaning in so far as it concerns him, and now he carries his rejoicings to the very limit of aggressiveness. Does it not occur to many an American of Anglo-Saxon parentage, when he watches an Italian, a Pole or a Greek noisily celebrating the "Fourth of July" that, after all, the great controversy of 1776 was a domestic affair of his own people, that it was fought out between two groups of his own ancestors? The war was waged on both sides of the ocean, it had begun more than a century before 1776, and some of its fundamental ideas have continued their battle ever since wherever Anglo-Saxons live. The joyful commemoration of those events by foreigners—who would shout equally loud and with equally scant understanding on Empire Day had they settled on the other side of the Canadian border—is at bottom a gross indiscretion, thoughtless horse-play with historical memories, which in their tragical greatness are a sacred inheritance of the Anglo-Saxon race. Should, however, any American of Anglo-Saxon extraction dare to protest against these foreigners setting themselves up as judges over his ancestors and history, the Legend of the Revolution, ossified, dried, cut up, distributed in the form of saintly relics among many shrines, is there to weigh on him and inhibit his actions. Yes, these foreigners can forbid him to call his blood, kin and ancestry his own, because he himself renounced them in a moment of bitter domestic feud a hundred and forty years ago. Men who remain wholly alien to him in mind and soul can claim a voice in his national councils and can lay hands on his national institutions. Can he stop them from doing so on the ground that they do not understand the true spirit of his civic inheritance? Steuben, Kosciuszko and Pulaski will be at once flung in his face, and rightly. For how much of the revolutionary conflict was understood by the patron saints and mythological forerunners of the recent immigrants? And yet their help was accepted, their memory is glorified, the cosmopolitan mark was received, and Englishry was renounced.

I was standing on the night of one "Fourth of July" in the Town Square of New Haven, which the first Puritan settlers had laid out centuries ago, on the steps of the Centre Church, which two Oxford men had founded. They had come here in order that they might realise their cherished dreams of the Puritan Commonwealth. Here English religious individualism had tried in congregations to work out its destiny, undisturbed by the contrary element within its own nation, untouched by the influence of its spiritual brethren of different nationality. In those surroundings I had dreamt many a time of the Puritan founders of the State, I had followed their paths among the wooded hills up the Connecticut River, I felt their thoughts when, on my pilgrimage, I reached the slopes near New Guildford, which, after long search, a group of immigrants from Surrey and Kent had chosen for their settlement, because it reminded them so much of the countryside of Southern England. It was impossible to think of that distant past in the Town Square of New Haven on the night of the " Fourth of July." A noisy, surging crowd was rolling through the square, rockets were fired, flags were waved. I heard Italian, French, Polish and Greek spoken around me. I saw hundreds of little American flags, and coupled with them flags of many nations. The one flag which was nowhere to be seen was that of Britain, the land which once had been loved as the mother country, which now is honoured by Americans as the centre of the great sister-commonwealth, but which on the " Fourth of July " is dimly thought of by the multi-lingual crowd in the New Haven Square as a brutal tyrant. What associations were rising in the imaginations of those in the crowd who had themselves suffered in the Old World, when they heard the phrases about " Britain's cruel yoke " ?

Across the square, in a fine old frame-house, I had sat at dinner that night with descendants of the founders of the State, with Anglo-Saxons of the purest lineage, in their feelings and thinking more closely allied to Englishmen than are millions of men now living under the British flag. We had sat behind drawn blinds, and a feeling of bored, weary uneasiness had seemed to prevail in the room. The noise was coming from outside, the Mob's Carnival was proceeding in the Square; I guessed that hardly any one of my companions, whose forefathers had been actors in the great drama, exactly knew what his own feelings now were towards the queer festivities of commemoration, or towards their still queerer participants, who by their very joy tried to let the old Americans know and feel that they were fellow-citizens. Did not the old Americans resent the indiscretion of the strange yelling and noisy rejoicings? In many of them flowed the blood of loyalists. Why were those Dagoes shouting over Hutchinson's broken heart, over Galloway's shattered life, over the mute tragedy of many of America's noblest men, over the "pity and fear" of the great Anglo-Saxon tragedy? Well, the fathers of the now "submerged Americans" used to celebrate that day before these strangers had entered the land; the rejoicings of the "Fourth of July" had grown to be the custom of the country. Could an American of Anglo-Saxon extraction now protest against them, against the Legend of the Revolution? Could he step forward and tell the foreign immigrants that the ideas of right and liberty, which *his* ancestors had brought over from the British Isles, were not dead in their old home, that each of the two great divisions of Anglo-Saxondom, treading its own path, had reached a freedom and developed a form of commonwealth unequalled by any other nation; that the attitude of the immigrants towards his own blood, kin and ancestry was offensive to him?

The same night I walked among the crowd with a descendant of the first Puritan settlers. I could guess the thoughts with which he was struggling; there were things which neither he nor I could formulate and neither of us would have dared to touch upon. We had left the Square, had passed out of the crowd, and were walking up a side road, between the mighty rows of old elm trees. Finally he broke the silence; he remarked with a smile, simulating cheerfulness: "We teach more foreigners English than does Great Britain, we compel them to adopt our language, laws and constitution in a way unknown to the British Empire." The Englishman spoke in him; there was not a drop of blood in him which was not the best blood of England. I felt like asking him why he did not unfurl the flag of his own ancestors and make the strangers in the Square and all their little foreign flags bow to it? Of course, they would shriek "Treason"; for could the glorious Revolution ever be forgotten, or interpreted in any other than the traditional way?

They were rejoicing in the Town Square over his renunciation of Englishry.

THE DISINHERITANCE OF AMERICA

(" *The Nation and Athenæum*," January 26th, 1929)

I once talked to an American girl about the Anglo-Saxons in America, how they alone dare not show any feeling for the name and the flag of their original home, and would be pilloried by their hyphenated fellow-citizens did they choose to forget the renunciation of Englishry which they made one hundred and fifty years ago. She protested passionately: " It is not we who have renounced England, England has renounced us. We keep returning, and produce amazing reasons for it. We want to shoot grouse, and there are none in America; we want to give parties, and don't like them dry. We invent a hundred futile excuses. The fact is, we want to come to England; and when we do, we are sneered at and treated as strangers."

Granted she is not typical of America, and, in fact, not even of her own family; some of them, of equally pure Anglo-Saxon lineage, travel all over Europe, but, in sullen hatred, refuse to visit England. Still, what is that if not an inverted, but almost equally telling, proof of their " family fixation" on this country? Why should they avoid the land of their ancestors, geographically the nearest to them, the country whose language they speak? Can this still be an after-effect of "the Boston tea-party" of December 1773? Does it not suggest some enduring source of irritation, an invisible tie which survives against their will and even without their knowing, and, in a hidden manner, hampers, hurts and provokes them—a persisting bondage?

We may note the explanations usually given for anti-British feeling in America. History as hitherto taught in American schools—but why should intelligent, self-respecting people have suffered so long nonsensical insults to be offered to their nearest kinsmen, and even to their own ancestors? For of the Anglo-Saxon ancestors of present-day Americans, in 1783 at least half were still on this side of the water. "The melting-pot"—" many races have gone to make this nation." Hysteria is "a somatic conversion of psychic facts," and the claim to alien ancestry raised on behalf of the American nation is an attempt to provide a somatic explanation for a mental attitude. Moreover, the claim is raised for the nation only, while the individual American, when tracing his own family, dwells by preference on his British ancestors, and does not eagerly search for immigrants from Eastern or Southern

Europe among his forefathers, though their blood would most clearly distinguish him from Englishmen, and most effectively obliterate the stigma of Englishry; an admixture of Irish, German, Scandinavian, Dutch, French or Jewish blood Englishmen have no less than Americans. Nor is it the " unmelting foreigner " who produces the alienation from England, however much he may be interested in its existence. When insults are hurled at England, the man's name is Thompson, not Tomasini or Tomashevich. Poor " Big Bill "!—it requires no psycho-analyst to discover that his vision of King George V. at Chicago was an inverted, subconscious declaration of allegiance. Were he of German, Italian or Slav extraction, the idea would not have occurred to him, but his disordered English thoughts straggled back into his repressed English past, and, however much circumstances or accidents may have contributed to it, the racial background of his vision is indelibly marked. It is that English past, neither ingested nor overcome, neither revived nor dead, which poisons the American mind with regard to England.

The relation of man to earth, of which he is and to which he returns, the mysterious bond between him and his native land, gives rise to curious social conceptions. Communities are personified by the name of the country they inhabit; a parental character is ascribed to the community which continues in the original territory as against the colonies, its "children"; and conscious historic continuity in communities largely depends on an unbroken connexion (be it merely ideal or sentimental) with a definite territory. The joint result was, and remains, perhaps the most important disturbing factor in Anglo-American relations.

In the eighteenth century England and America were primarily territorial conceptions. Englishmen and Americans were not Spartans and helots, inhabiting one territory, but separated by an invisible barrier, which individuals could not cross. Specific political advantages were connected with residence in this island, and were acquired by Americans on landing in Great Britain, and given up by Britons migrating to the Colonies. John Huske, Barlow Trecothick, Henry Cruger, Staats Long Morris, and Paul Wentworth, all five Americans, came over to England and sat in the British Parliament in the crucial period of 1761–83, while Tom Paine and William Gordon, absolute newcomers to America, were foremost among her spokesmen in the conflict with England. When "America" and "England" are discussed in history, one does not think about the actual individuals who composed the two communities, and territorial descriptions are treated as if the human element covered by them had been constant. Thus even Americans, whose families did not migrate till the nineteenth century, and who therefore in 1783 came under the designation of England and not of America, still speak as if they had shared in the supposed indignities of Colonial dependence. But the easier it is for individuals to pass from one group to the other, the more imperative it becomes for them to ascribe reality to territorial denominations.

In the discussions of 1764–76 England and the Colonies are continually personified as the Mother Country and its " offspring," the parent who ought to be tender and lenient, and the children who should be affectionate, dutiful and obedient; and one feels relieved when Benjamin Franklin, a scientist and not an historian, at last asks the obvious question, whether a young Englishman is the father of an elderly American, and whether grey hair in the Colonies is less venerable than in Great Britain ? And yet, if a man thinks himself the Emperor of China, there must be some subjectively valid reason for such a fantasy, and when whole communities are obsessed by a delusion, there must be something in it which is individually normal.

Moreover, this particular delusion was not peculiar to eighteenth-century Anglo-Saxons. In the dispute between Corinth and Corcyra, according to Thucydides, the Corcyreans declared that they had not gone forth to be slaves, and the "parental" Corinthians replied that they had not nurtured the infant colony to be insulted afterwards; by two thousand years they forestalled the argument of 1776. Indeed, a fetishism of places is universally human, and was reproduced even by those who are sometimes alleged to have been reborn with a new consciousness, when they touched American soil. In 1634, a few years after Watertown in Massachusetts had been founded, part of the colonists left it and settled at Weathersfield; but when divisions occurred in the new congregation, according to Trumbull, "the church at Watertown, as they had not dismissed their brethren at Weathersfield from their watch, judged it their duty to make them a visit, and to attempt to heal the divisions." Similar action on the part of the Weathersfield would probably have been considered uncalled-for, and even insolent—a few years' difference sufficed to establish a family hierarchy.

The idea of "young nations" to some extent explains the origin of that hierarchy. What is it that makes nations young or old, and how can a nation be either? A friend, more than twenty years my senior, hearing me speak of the Jews as the oldest of nations, impatiently protested that all mankind was coeval. "Would you, then, say," I replied," that we two are the same age, because the matter of which we consist is coeval?" The age of men and nations alike is in the length of conscious continuity. Anchored in the Bible and the Promised Land, we Jews look back at three thousand years of a national existence focused on one idea. The historic consciousness of the Englishman extends over a thousand years, as far back as his churches and churchyards take him—" *ce qui fait la patrie, ce sont les autels des dieux et les tombeaux des ancêtres.*" But what about the Americans? As an idea, untrue of at least 90 per cent. of them, they extend their historic consciousness over three hundred years; if they go further back, their thoughts carry them to England, the Mother Country of the Anglo-Saxon community in America, not the native land of the individual American Anglo-Saxon; it is anterior to America, older than his present homeland. Were England in ruins, dead and uninhabited, it would be a holy shrine to Americans. But this island continued its own development, and the England of the American emigrants has not acted, either in life or death, the personified part of a " mother." The kinsmen who have stayed behind are now seated in the place of the common ancestors; they have an individuality of their own, and yet identify themselves with these ancestors, and in a way impersonate them. A very complex psychological situation has arisen; those kinsmen seem to monopolise the common inheritance; it adds to their self-conscious dignity; the present-day Englishman seems to stand between the American and his own past.

It is this which makes, at least some, Americans feel that they have been "renounced" by England. They are strangers in the land which is their ancestral home no less than of present-day Englishmen (and more so than of some who have since entered it). They have left it one, two or three centuries ago; they may have been actuated by economic considerations, or driven out by political or religious dissensions, or they may have gone as a matter of choice, from a sense of adventure. They have done well for their descendants; these are now prosperous, rich—much richer than their English cousins. And yet—their historic birthright—is compensation for it to be found in gold? With gold they try to regain at least some of the inheritance. They buy mediæval manuscripts, Shakespeare folios, English pictures; they want the bones of General Oglethorpe; they transfer historic buildings, carefully marking the stones, so as to reconstruct them accurately on the other side; they try to re-acquire bodily a piece of their own past and set it up in their new homes. They pay fantastic prices for the manuscript of " Alice in Wonderland," and argue that Mary who had a lamb was an American—a symbolic attempt to Americanise their " childhood." The manifestations of their craving to regain their " lost shadow " are sometimes grotesque, but there are human feeling and unconscious suffering in them; the historic tragedy engenders bitterness. No corresponding development is noticeable among the German-Americans, or the American Scandinavians, Czechs, Poles, etc., not even among the Scottish settlers in America, or the English settlers in the Argentine. For none of them have created a new political entity in their own terms; there is no interplay of territorial conceptions. The original attachment may be extinguished, but is never inverted into bitterness; for such differences arise on a group basis only.

The great mass of Americans who in the past roamed about an empty Continent had little historic sense, and so have those who to this day form America's floating population. One has to be normally static to have a normal perception of movement. For Americans, until recently, time did not seem to flow. So far from living at a quicker pace than other nations, even the historically minded used to jumble up the past with the present—to them it was all on one plane; I knew an American who felt deeply about the "bar-sinister" of his English ancestor in the fifteenth century. But the more the Americans (and also the younger Dominions) attain stability and become conscious of their historic continuity, the more they will reach back to their English past; and the moral and psychological problem will increase in importance: how that English past, which is the common inheritance of all Anglo-Saxons, can be made truly common to them all, for Englishmen are its trustees rather than its sole heirs.

Unless family relations are exceedingly good, it is hard to bear the apparent superiority with which "the fetishism of places" endows those in possession of the original home. The break between England and America came, not as a revolt against real "oppression"—excessive importance must not be attached to the American fears of being "enslaved" by means of stamps or of a tea-duty; such catastrophes are common wherever Anglo-Saxons play at politics and are called upon to pay taxes (when, in 1645, Connecticut tried to impose a small duty at Saybrook, on the Connecticut River, Massachusetts protested that this duty would "necessarily enslave their posterity," and when, in 1754, an Excise Act was passed by Massachusetts, Plymouth declared that this would not merely "destroy the natural rights of every private family, but also of each individual in the Government "). The revolt was against the superiority assumed by those who stayed behind. The bonds remained close, and there was no real estrangement in the sense of feeling alien to each other. In June, 1774, Charles Thomson wrote to Samuel Adams:

> "Would to God they all, even our enemies, knew the warm attachment we have for Great Britain, notwithstanding we have been contending these ten years with them for our rights."

There was the common spiritual treasure in the Mother Country, and Americans expected to share in it for all time, or, indeed, to become its main heirs. William Hooper wrote about Great Britain on January 6th, 1776, half a year before he signed the Declaration of Independence as a representative of North Carolina:—

> "Oh Heaven! Still check her approaching ruin; restore her to the affection of her American subjects. May she long flourish as the guardian of freedom, and whenever the change comes, and come it must, that America must become the seat of Empire, may Britain gently verge down the decline of life and sink away in the arms of American sons."

How much is told in these few lines! The idea of the " Mother Country " and her " children " is pushed to its logical conclusion—as children grow up, the parents become old and weak, which analogy about 1770 produced the belief in America that Great Britain was rapidly declining. The status of " subjects " is implicitly accepted, and the character of " the guardian of freedom " is attributed as natural to Great Britain. And the final conclusion is that her inheritance is to pass to the Americans. In the unconscious depths, the bitterness which is still alive in Americans of pure Anglo-Saxon lineage over the Revolution does not refer to the incidents of 1774, nor even to the calamities of the war, but to the lasting exclusion of Americans from the common English inheritance. From this point of view it is indifferent whether the ancestors of the present-day American crossed the Atlantic before or after 1783.

All this may seem fantastic to Englishmen who know, and possibly have suffered from, the " man of Kansas "; still more so to that man himself. He may even feel insulted; it has never occurred to him that he wants to be English, or to look back across centuries to the churches and churchyards of England. And yet, whoever comes to see what the vision of King George at Chicago really means, will perhaps withhold judgment, and try to re-examine the unconscious foundations of

American mentality. That striving back—not so much to present-day England, but to the common past—which appears, positive and crystallised, in many modern American historians and in the most cultured Americans, exists, be it in an unconscious or still more often in a negative form, in the mind of the average Anglo-Saxon American. The very heat and passion with which he reacts to the name and idea of England are an eloquent proof of their not being indifferent to him.

PUBLIC OPINION AND REPRESENTATIVE GOVERNMENT

(" *The Nation and Athenæum*," September 15th, 1928)

SHELBURNE wrote in 1801, after more than forty years spent in the forefront of politics :—

> " People talk of public opinion ; and what creates or constitutes public opinion ? Numbers certainly do not."

Where is it to be found ? And how is it to be ascertained ? How many people hold clear, articulate views even about the most important national concerns ? And if their views are original and well-grounded, what chance is there of their being representative ? Statesmen trying to ascertain the state of " public opinion " present indeed a pathetic sight. Here is the picture which Sir Robert Morier drew of Mr. Gladstone's Government on the outbreak of the Franco-Prussian War in 1870 :—

> " . . . the Ministry is going about asking here and asking there what public opinion wishes. I heard how Gladstone went about on the steamer of the Cobden Club, collecting opinions from individual members

like a monkey asking for ha'pence, asking this one if he really believed England would be ready to go to war, that one whether he considered England's honour engaged in Belgium, etc., etc. . . ."

Nor would Sir Robert Morier, though a man of fundamentally liberal views, admit that the Press could be considered as expressive of public opinion; that conception was to him "the thoroughly rotten . . . partnership now established between the so-called Executive (! !) and the so-called public opinion. . . ." He wrote to Lord Russell on November 7th, 1870:—

> "The leaders of the people sitting in Whitehall and Downing Street call to the leaders of the people sitting in editorial chairs in Printing House Square and the back slums of the Strand for ideas wherewith to be inspired; the gentlemen of the scissors and glue-pot return the compliment. . . . It is impossible to tell which is the voice and which is the echo. Is the leader in the *Daily Telegraph* the vulgarised reverberation of what Mr. Gladstone had told Mr. Levi, or is Mr. Gladstone's speech at the Soapboilers' Superannuation Society a classicised version of the instructions Mr. Levi has given in the morning to Mr. Gladstone? Who can tell —no one can tell—neither Mr. Levi nor Mr. Gladstone; they are both of them burning incense to an unknown God. . . ."

That god remains unknown; he is not to be found in any definable shape in any definite quarter, he is not heard speaking in articulate terms, but his presence is felt as all-pervading. "Numbers" do not make public opinion; numbers cannot give the directive for particular political decisions; numbers cannot be consulted on such matters; numbers do not consider what road should be taken until the consequences of the decision are brought home to them. What was British "public opinion" during the American Revolution? And how could it have been ascertained? In 1774, after ten years of discussions of the colonial problem, on the eve of events unsurpassed in greatness by anything since the break-up of the Roman dominions into a Western and an Eastern Empire, not a single election in Great Britain was turned, or even influenced to any marked extent, by the American issue; but the consequences of the American Revolution have produced a clearly defined attitude in Great Britain with regard to British settlements overseas. Now the problem of the "Dark Empire" is with us, unsolved, demanding a solution, fraught with incalculable consequences, infinitely more complex and difficult than what now seems to us the very simple problem of the First British Empire. Possibly we are laying the foundations of a new type of Empire, or possibly, by doing too much or too little, we are destroying another British Empire. But how many of us hold a clear, articulate view on the subject? Was ever a general election, or even a by-election, seriously affected by the question of the policy to be adopted in India? If a conflict imposed heavy sacrifices on us, an opinion would make itself felt in favour of persevering, or of cutting losses. We develop opinions when called upon to act, to fight, or to pay; then we are anxious, ready, or loath to do so, or, in most cases, to continue doing so. But there can be no public opinion with regard to things so delicate as a policy to be pursued, still less to particular measures to be adopted.

The framework of our political life now rests on organised parties. By consulting the Whips, a leader may learn how the rank and file of his party in the House is likely to react to certain measures or proposals. But neither the Whips nor their wards can be relied upon to interpret correctly the inarticulate, incoherent words of the "unknown god" who talks in his sleep. As for party organisations in the constituencies, they are certain to voice nothing but the most biased, the most intransigent and the most hackneyed party views; they consist primarily of men strong in the faith, zealous for the cause, therefore unreceptive of delicate changes in atmosphere, and unrepresentative of those on the fringes of the party and in the middle regions between parties, who are easiest turned and who turn the scales by their weight on the margin. Political propagandists make a poor political barometer. Moreover, if asked for an independent opinion, the professionalised politicians are likely to remain mute, and finally to decide on grounds alien to the problem—the party organisation stands in the centre of their " political " thinking, and its problems will in most cases determine their decision. An account of how the first great party machine built up in this country failed its maker, Mr. Joseph Chamberlain, and misled its leader, Mr. Gladstone, is given by M. Ostrogorski in his book on " Democracy and the Organisation of Political Parties " :—

> " On the eve of the Home Rule debate in the House of Commons the Liberal Federation Committee requested all the affiliated Associations to consider the question and to forward it the resolutions which they might adopt. . . . The Federation, realising the division of opinion, confined itself on this occasion, contrary to its usual practice, to a simple statement of the problem. . . . Left to their own inspiration, the Associations for the most part did not know what line to take. They who were supposed to have the power of giving expression to public opinion

and of pointing out the policy to be pursued by their rulers, could do nothing but stammer. . . . And it was left to Mr. Chamberlain to utter the feeling cry: ' Why are you here? Why are you formed? Why do you remain an Association for Birmingham?' "

When the delegates met at the Westminster Palace Hotel their veneration for Mr. Gladstone was " reinforced by all the animosity, jealousy and rancour which had gathered round the Birmingham set," who " had not been able or willing to spare the *amour-propre* of the other towns." Under the leadership of the Leeds contingent, they excommunicated Mr. Chamberlain and his men; and Mr. Gladstone was led to believe that the party was solid behind him.

As for the impression which any one of us obtains from his own scrutiny of " public opinion," it can deceive none but the most uncritical among us. Henry Cruger, a New York merchant settled at Bristol and representing the city in Parliament, wrote on March 21st, 1775, to Ralph Izard, a South Carolina planter: " . . . the people of this country, I mean the merchants, take so warm a part against administration . . ."; and Edward Gibbon, the historian, seeing consciously what Cruger perceived in a subconscious manner, and enjoying the humour of it, wrote on February 23rd, 1778: " I do not find that the World, that is, a few people whom I happen to converse with, are much inclined to praise Lord N[orth]'s ductility of temper. . . ." The few people we "happen to converse with" are necessarily to us "the people of this country" and constitute its "public opinion."

Anyone who has ever taken part in a political movement knows what "resolutions" are worth, how a seemingly powerful campaign in the Press can be started by a few able and zealous writers, how a stage army can be marched out by one door and brought back by another, and how the appearances of an "opinion" can be created (and also how quickly and easily they peter out once the management is withdrawn). Everyone knows how elections are made, how issues can be manipulated, how little of a mandate for particular purposes is obtained from general elections, and how easy it is to deceive oneself and mistake the echo of one's own cries and enthusiasms for a spontaneous, intelligent voice. And still—after all is said that can be said in ridicule of the conception of a "public opinion" and of the methods employed with a view to ascertaining it, the fact remains that it exists, and that it forms the best part of those "circumstances" which both Frederick the Great and Napoleon recognised as their master. There is such a thing as a logic of ideas, and ideas, when looked at from a distance, seem to have an independent life and existence of their own; their " logic " is the outcome of the slow, hardly conscious thinking of the masses, very primitive, simplified in the process of accumulation, and in its mass advance deprived of all individual features, like the pebbles in a river-bed. And there is such a thing as a mental atmosphere, which at times becomes so all-pervading that hardly anyone can withdraw himself from its influence.

It is the avowed aim of our system of representative and responsible government to secure the rule of " public opinion," and it does so to a fairly satisfactory degree, provided no ill-judged attempts are made at attaining accuracy by narrow, artificial, mechanical devices, which cannot supply reliable results, but merely produce a deceptive feeling of knowledge and certainty, where watchful attention and conscientious searching of heart more nearly answer the purpose. However fine a machine proportional representation, referendums, popular initiative, etc., may be, they cannot supply a valid verdict where there is no articulate thought, and they moreover rest on, and in turn foster, the dangerous delusion that public opinion is a matter of numbers. Votes can only be counted, not weighed, and the degree of emphasis which the individual puts into his vote, the measure of sacrifice with which he is prepared to back it, and the dynamic force of his personality, are hopelessly lost in this purely mechanical process. The " unknown god " cannot be measured with a tape.

The true ideal of representative government is to place men in office who are likely to react to problems, situations and events in the same way as the great mass of their countrymen, only to do so first and in a more articulate and deliberate manner than the masses can; this is called leadership. In other words, the rulers, if properly chosen, should be able to find the directive of public opinion in their own consciousness and feelings; and if they fail to find it there, they are not likely to ascertain it correctly by any other means. Elections and Parliament do not primarily serve the purpose of determining public opinion in arithmetical terms; they constitute an elaborate system of political tests which, like Civil Service examinations, are irrelevant in most of their apparent searchings, and yet fundamentally effective. The capacity for expressing in an articulate form that which germinates in the minds of other people, and for co-operating with other men, is continually tested in British public life.

Undoubtedly most dictators have public opinion behind them when they first seize power, and they usually plead this for their excuse. But dictatorships offer no possibility for change or for a free renewal of the mandate; they realise the precept which Machiavelli gives to prophets, to acquire power while men believe in them, so as to be able to enforce faith after it is gone. It is change which constitutes the very nature of representative and responsible government, and, curiously enough, under the present system of party politics, the chances of change decrease with the arithmetical accuracy of election returns, for the great mass of the electorate always votes the same way, and changes occur only in a narrow margin, whose oscillations acquire under our present system a conveniently disproportionate importance. At this time, when Parliamentary government breaks down in most countries which have adopted it in a mechanically perfected form, it is most essential to preserve its organic, though illogical, foundations. Fundamentally our Government is " representative " in the same way as a jury; it consists of men who react, or are supposed to react, in a typical, representative manner. The rest is an elaborate, sometimes naive, often mismanaged, but on the whole effective, machinery for selection and change, and one of the most valuable features of the system is the conscious uncertainty about things that can never be accurately ascertained; which uncertainty, in prudent and honest minds, produces caution.

THE BIOGRAPHY OF ORDINARY MEN

(" *The Nation and Athenæum*," *July 14th,* 1928)

STUDY-circles of working men, when asked what subject they would like to take, almost invariably answer with a request for " economic history." Political history, they reason, is about kings and statesmen and wars, while they want to learn about " the likes " of themselves—as all the other classes and professions did before them. But how much of that desire is satisfied by stories about the enclosures, the spinning-jenny, the Poor Law, the Factory Acts or the Free Trade controversy? Students are landed once more in the sphere of legislative enactments and of Government measures ; for these are " documented " and can be easily dished up, whereas the tale of those ordinary men and women about whom they want to know is buried in casual remarks, in crevices of unknown texts—pins in haystacks. In the correspondence of the upper classes remarks occasionally occur which throw a flood of light on the life and condition of " the lower orders," but will anyone ever collect and blend them into a picture ? Why, even a history of the rank and file of what may best be their fortunes and now aspired to social advancement, Civil Servants, lawyers and political wire-pullers who tried to raise their professional status, etc. The rise of " interests " and classes can be traced through the personnel of the House of Commons, the forms of English gregarious existence can be studied, the social structure of England is reflected in it, the presence or decay of independent political life in boroughs and counties can be watched in their representation. When the sons of peers or leading country gentlemen begin to invade the representation of boroughs, it is clear that Parliament is becoming the governing body; when the brewers, clothiers and ironmasters start acquiring seats in the House, it is obvious that fortunes are being made in these branches of trade, and that the early capitalists have made their appearance; by the number of West Indians in the House one can measure the prosperity of the "sugar islands"; when many families of country gentlemen, who for generations had sat in it, withdraw from the House of Commons, one can guess that agricultural rents are falling—on a careful inquiry it will be found that the coming in of American wheat has wrought a greater change in the composition of the British House of Commons than the first two Reform Acts. From the " circular letter," the whip which in the eighteenth century was sent to Government profitably attempted unless one writes the history of a crowd. It would not pay to go through hundreds of volumes of manuscripts and many thousands of books merely to fish out some twenty documents or passages about one man. Proper returns cannot be obtained from the work except by following up many threads, by establishing the average and selecting the typical. The student has to get acquainted with the lives of thousands of individuals, with an entire ant-heap, see its files stretch out in various directions, understand how they are connected and correlated, watch the individual ants, and yet never forget the ant-heap. An interesting piece of research into economic history could be done by studying the lives of the members of any great trading company in the seventeenth and eighteenth centuries, or, say, of the directing personnel of the East India House. But most of all there is that marvellous microcosmos of English social and political life, that extraordinary club, the House of Commons. For centuries it has been the goal of English manhood, and besides those who found seats in it on the strength of a tradition or of a quasi-hereditary right, there were in every House many scores of men, for whom its membership set the crown (and often the coronet) on achievements and success in other walks of life. Generals, admirals and proconsuls entered it, business men who had made in a sceptical, would-be humorous, depreciatory manner, and this is the main tangible expression of the doubt which besets the writers as to whether these men truly deserve the prominence they receive. The outstanding figures are reduced to ordinary dimensions, but continue to fill the picture, mainly because information about them can be easily obtained. Still, what can one expect from the lonely student, not given even the most elementary help (*e.g.*, of a secretary or an assistant to do for him some of the more mechanical work) or the necessary leisure for his researches, as usually he is compelled to earn his living by teaching? Is he to attempt to cross an ocean in a boat of the most primitive construction? Our interests and requirements have changed and broadened, we want to know about the life of crowds, to hear symphonies and not arias, and then a single virtuoso is invited to perform them. Occasionally we take refuge in collective works, and fondly expect "fifty men to make a centipede"; more often than not, these attempts at joint and yet individual work end in failure. Historical research to this day remains unorganised, and the historian is expected to make his own instruments or do without them; and so with wooden ploughs we continue to draw lonely furrows, most successfully when we strike sand.

The biography of the ordinary man cannot be

described as "the political nation" is seldom attempted; biographies of famous men still hold the field, though hero-worship is no longer the creed of the writers. But, then, a biography has well-defined limits, a natural sequence and an established practice, and can be compiled by an individual writer in a reasonably short time; nor is it attempted unless materials are ready to hand. Lastly, the public is accustomed to read biographies, and so they continue to be produced.

In biographies, as in plays, the central figures act and speak, the others being mere dummies in the background, "citizens," "soldiers," etc. In most cases the biographer does not profess an exclusive interest in the psychology of his "hero" and would not deny the importance of the men who surround him; and yet they remain a dark, dumb, nameless crowd. We have written about Parliamentary leaders and great administrators, and more or less ignored those whom they led and with or through whom they had to do their work, the individual Members of Parliament, the Civil Servants, etc. We have written about changes in methods of production, the rise of modern finance, trade statistics, but very seldom about the men behind these developments, the merchants who turned manufacturers or bankers, the land-owners who became mining adventurers, etc. Now the heroes of biography are often approached

Members at the opening of the session, one can learn a good deal about political groupings; about 1750, independent country gentlemen sitting "in their own right" received it usually from the leader of the House, relatives or retainers of politically prominent peers through them, members of professional groups through their chiefs (naval officers through the First Lord of the Admiralty, lawyers through the Lord Chancellor, Government contractors and financiers through the Secretary to the Treasury, etc.), and lastly, in one or two cases, territorial managers made their appearance.

We have discussed kings and statesmen and wars, and when desirous to show our appreciation of "progress"—institutions, inventions and "reforms." But how much do we know about the real political life of the country, even about that body which before the eyes of the nation has for centuries shaped its joint existence? How much do we know about the Members of the Long Parliament, or about the changes which came over the House between the accession of George III. and the voting of the First Reform Act? When did local citizens disappear from the representation of most small provincial boroughs? When did rich City merchants begin to plant themselves out on them? When did provincial business men of the new type start entering the House in considerable numbers? When did national politics become the dominant issue in elections? When and how have parties got the upper hand over individual candidates? When was the loyalty of the average elector transferred from organic constituencies to party organisations? In the eighteenth century as many excuses had to be made for "disturbing the peace" of a county or borough as in our time for starting a war, and every candidate in an election contest naturally tried to prove that it was not he who was the aggressor, but that his opponent, by an inexcusable disregard of his "just pretensions," had forced a contest on him, in which he himself confidently relied on the fairness of his neighbours to secure his victory. The idea that constituencies should be contested for the political education of the electorate was as alien to the eighteenth century as would be to us a proposal that the summer manœuvres of our army should take the form of a three-days' battle with that of some other nation. Even about the middle of the nineteenth century, in a good many constituencies the local issues still predominated, and, *e.g.*, the Radicals could form an almost separate body in the House without producing any considerable number of triangular contests, for the battle was not fought on a national scale. Without underrating the value of work on what is called the political history of the British nation, one might wish that at least a start should be made with a history of the British " political nation." And a biographical history of the House of Commons, covering the seven centuries of its existence, could well supply the spade-work for such a new venture along lines consonant with the general change in our outlook and interests.

Parliamentary histories based on the biographies of Members have been attempted for various counties, and much of this work has been done by real scholars. Useful as these books undoubtedly are, they suffer from the following of " vertical " lines—what has Adam Fitz-Richard, returned for Liverpool in 1295, in common with some big merchant of the eighteenth century, or with George Canning who represented Liverpool 1812–23 ? By taking counties or single constituencies, one can study, *e.g.*, the degree of heredity in their representation, but one touches merely the outskirts of political life, and cannot properly follow up the personal connections even of the Members in question, for these extended in most cases far beyond the borders of their constituency or county. Much better results could be reached by doing the work " horizontally "—an attempt of that kind seems to have been planned by Mr. Pink, one of the greatest antiquaries of our time, who collected biographical material about the Members of the Long Parliament, but died without having published anything on the subject. The student of Parliamentary biography whose work is limited to one period, but extends over the entire country, can do what is impossible for those working on vertical lines—he can plunge into the mass of manuscript and printed material extant for his period and obtain from it a living picture of the men. Still, no such study of one single period can fully realise its aim unless similar studies, on the same plan, are available for other periods; only by comparison can we gauge movement and correctly define its nature.

In short, the task cannot be undertaken by individual researchers, working independently of each other. It has to be organised on a national scale, given national standing, and financed from national resources. A central organisation is required, an editorial board composed of experts and working under the auspices of a Parliamentary Committee, co-operating with various county organisations, with bodies such as the editors of " The Complete Peerage," with scholars working on the biographies of members of universities, colleges or schools, with other experts specialising in cognate subjects. "A Dictionary of Parliamentary Biography" should be compiled, but based on periods, and not on the alphabet. The entity and individuality of consecutive Houses have to be clearly preserved, for the pageant of history must not be arranged under capital letters, like the luggage on the pier at Liverpool. The value of such work executed on a sufficiently large scale and according to the highest standards of scholarship could hardly be exaggerated. It would be a " Who's Who " of politics and social life throughout the ages, the most indispensable reference book for everyone engaged on English political history and for every editor of historical manuscripts—and it would save us from having to do the same work over and over again, often without sufficient means or knowledge. But of equal or perhaps even greater importance would be the attempt inherent in that work to organise historical research, and last, but not least, the training which the work would give to younger collaborators. It is difficult to imagine a better preparation for history work on any given period than a study of the lives of the men of that time, in the course of which a proper knowledge of the available materials would naturally be acquired.

COMMUNITIES

(" *The Nation and Athenæum*," December 3rd, 1927)

At the passages of Jordan the men of Gilead slew forty-two thousand Ephraimites for reasons much better than the modern derisive use of the word "shibboleth" would seem to suggest. "Art thou an Ephraimite?" was the basic question; they tried to ascertain each man's "community," the invisible bonds which are as real as man's own existence, and, indeed, dominate it.

Every test becomes a shibboleth when the reality of that which it was to have tested, or the organic connection between them, is felt no more. By an enormous effort some reflection in words is found for relations of human life; but symbols, when repeated, tend to become decorative, and as words gain currency, their rich, living contents gradually fade away. The schematic conceptions which remain, clothed with a seemingly independent existence, draw men into misinterpreting themselves and misunderstanding each other. History, when viewed in terms of pure ideas, becomes a record of human folly. But men are seldom so absurd as words make them appear;

seldom, if ever, do they fight and die, or even kill, for a mere shibboleth.

To some the subject-matter of medicine is disease, and of history ideas, as if these were extraneous things which visit or befall human beings. But disease is merely a condition of the human body defined and circumscribed by medical thought, and some diseases vanish, whilst others appear, only because of changes in medical conceptions and terminology. Nor have nationality and religions an independent existence and permanent, immutable contents; they reflect certain things in the lives of communities, and often the same things under changed names. When dominant and contested, they denote the existence of different communities which acknowledge no bond higher than their own internal bond, and fight over the eternal, insoluble problem how mass organisms can co-exist within the same or contiguous territory. Community, however, is a living reality, which merely centres and finds its symbol in some acknowledged principle or combination of principles—consanguinity, real or presumed; the profession of a creed; the use of a language; the manner of securing one's livelihood. But in the consciousness of men, communal existence and inter-communal conflicts assume a tribal, religious, national or class character; until at last it appears as if the particular distinguishing principle had created those communities and given origin to their conflicts. In reality a mass organism can be called by a dozen names, and every principle which arises from it, and by which it happens to be distinguished, stands for much more than its visible contents. It expresses the nature of the community, and is all-pervading.

"Division in religion," declared Sir John Eliot in the House of Commons on June 23rd, 1625, "dissolves all ties and obligations, civil and natural, the observation of heaven being more powerful than either policy or blood." But when scanning the heavens, the Latin races found them essentially Roman; and the upper classes among the Anglo-Saxons deduced from such observation a form of religion more authoritarian, traditional and hierarchic than did the people, inclining in Presbyterian Scotland and Congregationalist New England towards Episcopalianism, and in Episcopalian England towards Catholicism. Like the mariners of those days, by a close and intense "observation of heaven" men discovered their exact position on the earth; for nine-tenths of religion bear on relations between men and not on creed. Individual souls seek God, but communities and classes express in religion their own nature and aims, and adorn or burden it with their own peculiar signs and symbols; and it is not God who makes creeds differ. When religion ceases to be the principle of division between communities, men soon discover that in every god there is something divine, and that the gods of various creeds are very nearly interchangeable.

"For my part, sir," declared Dr. Johnson, "I think all Christians, whether Papists or Protestants, agree in the essential articles, and that their differences are trivial, and rather political, than religious." But just because the differences are political, so long as the community seeks its supreme self-expression in religion, conformity is demanded from its members; and Johnson himself defended the regional principle in religion even where the differences were not trivial to him.

> "JOHNSON: The vulgar are the children of the State, and must be taught like children. BOSWELL: Then, sir, a poor Turk must be a Mohammedan, just as a poor Englishman must be a Christian? JOHNSON: Why, yes, sir; and what then? This now is such stuff as I used to talk to my mother when I first began to think myself a clever fellow; and she ought to have whipt me for it."

In England uniformity never received more than an external, political character; there was no prying into beliefs, overt acts alone were required and considered. When, under James I., Parliament demanded the enforcement of anti-Papist legislation, they emphasised that their intention was not to interfere with the souls of men—these must be left to the Lord—but merely to control the movement of the bodies. By communion with the Established Church, Englishmen were expected to signify their adherence and submission to the national community; they were to show their " common sense."

" Our religion," wrote William Cobbett, the Radical, two centuries later, about his family, " was that of the Church of England, to which I have ever remained attached; the more so, perhaps, as it bears the name of my country. . . ." The inherited, communal character of his religion was not a matter of offence to this thoroughly human, big-hearted man; he felt in it none of the reproach with which the zealot, Samuel Fothergill, described in 1754 the very sound and sensible condition of the Pennsylvania Quakers, who had a " profession of religion which was partly national, which descended like the patrimony, and cost as little."

Simple men subconsciously recognise and know the complex social character of religion. A friend of mine lives in a part of Eastern Europe where the landowners and peasants are Catholics, and the traders and artisans Jews, while the few rich Jews who enter the squirearchy become Catholics. On her estate there was, however, a poor Jew who worked as a farm labourer, and through a similar process of social assimilation finished as a convert. "Still, he was always such a Catholic," was the comment of another peasant for whom the mere fact of peasant labour qualified the Jew as a member of the Christian community. Not so for the cook at the manor-house, who, having been some thirty years in the family, felt akin to the ruling classes, and who had never seen Jewish "converts" except among the squirearchy: "I told the priest he should not baptize him, and I was sure your ladyship would share my view; baptism is not for such a simple, vulgar Jew." She thought, like some of the royalist aristocrats of the Faubourg St. Honoré on the conversion of a well-known Jewish journalist, that baptism should be reserved for Jews of higher social standing.

Religion, when it embodies the dominant social principle, does and must denote community; and it was one of the most ominous signs in Russia that the name of Christians (*krestyanye*) should have been limited by the peasants to themselves alone; the others were thus implicitly put beyond the bounds of community—the first step towards class-war. The stronger the bonds of community, the more indistinguishable are the various signs or symptoms of communal existence; hence the absurdity of discussing whether the Jews are a race, a nation, or a religious congregation—they are a community. Hence also among the most truly clannish of nations, the Scots, the national Church holds a peculiar position; a Scotsman, even if a perfect agnostic, retains a fine feeling of reverence for the Presbyterian Church and its organisation, because, at least subconsciously, he understands its national, communal character. For the same reason the Scots never showed much feeling or sympathy for their own co-religionaries among other nations, *e.g.*, for the English or American Presbyterians during the American Revolution. And when I once told a Scottish minister about a member of a Latin race who had become a Presbyterian and was preaching Presbyterianism to his countrymen—" Good Lord ! " was his only comment; the thing seemed to him, to say the least, highly unbecoming. But this did not prevent him from warmly contesting my thesis about the predominantly sociological, communal character of religion.

" Never has it happened that two or more nations should have the same god," says the fervent Christian, Dostoyevsky. " Each nation has its own God. It marks the decline of nations when they start sharing their gods. Then the gods die, and the faith dies together with the nations. The stronger the nation, the more exclusive is its God." A community must be distinctive in its most fervent and passionate tenets, or it ceases to be a community.

And when "nation shall not lift up sword against nation, neither . . . learn war any more," still they "will walk every one in the name of his God, and we will walk in the name of the Lord our God for ever and ever."

THE EUROPEAN SITUATION

(" *The American Leader*," New York, July 9th, 1914)

[I RETURNED from the U.S.A. to Europe in April 1914, and in May I set out for a short tour through Central and Eastern Europe. During that trip I gained the conviction that we were on the eve of a World War. I came back to London on June 6th and called on a friend at the Foreign Office to tell him about my fears; naturally I said much more than I would have ventured to record in print. Still, in the course of the next week I wrote the following article, stating that " Europe is proceeding with its preparations for the storm of our age, for the *détente* which seems to break over it in every second or third generation "; and I despatched the article to America about a fortnight before the Sarajevo murder. I prophesied correctly before the event!]

The man who, after a year's absence, now returns to Europe with the conception of her international relations, which he had carried away a year ago, cannot help being amazed at the profound changes that have occurred during that time in the European situation. It is true in the outward grouping of the Great Powers nothing seems to differ from what it was last year; we still find them divided into the two camps of the Triple Alliance and the Triple Entente. Nor has the tension between these two groups diminished in any way, nor has their competition in armaments become less fierce; on the contrary, in all the Continental States, the expenditure on armaments has, during the last year, increased to such a terrific height, that no regular taxation, however, heavy, can now meet the military requirements any longer and recourse has to be had to extraordinary levies and loans. Europe is proceeding with its preparations for the storm of our age, for the *détente* which seems to break over it in every second or third generation and by means of which the silent shifting of power, that proceeds from day to day as if it were underground, finds expression in a changed balance and grouping of States and nations.

The tension then in the European atmosphere has not diminished, but the storm-centre has shifted. It has moved from the West to the East of Europe. During the last seven or eight years the rivalry between England and Germany was looked upon as the danger-spot in the European situation. After Russia's defeat in Manchuria, after the moral victory of the Central European States in the Bosnian crisis of 1909, Germany and Austria seemed to have become the deciding factor on the European Continent. The apparent predominance of Germany, which was in reality largely due to the blunders committed by British diplomacy in 1909, received its first check in the Morocco crisis of 1911. That change was caused on the one hand by Austria's desertion of her ally (the Austro-Hungarian Foreign Office declared through the mouth of the Hungarian Premier that the Triple Alliance does not extend beyond Europe), on the other hand by the very firm position which England took on the side of France. Not less remarkable than England's decision to proceed even to extremities in support of France was the total self-effacement of Russia during the crisis. At the most threatening moment, when the British fleets were being prepared for action, Russia was moving regiments from the Prussian frontier to the Ural, thereby giving Germany a tangible pledge that she would not support her ally in case of war.

The Morocco crisis led to a very strong rise in the anti-British feeling in Germany. It was felt that, had it not been for England, France would have had to give in; but even had the French Government adopted the sharpest attitude, Germans would have understood their doing so in their own cause. They could not forgive England having done it in a matter which did not seem to affect her directly, and the idea got hold both of the official and the "popular" mind in Germany that England was playing "the dog in the manger" and that the only way for

Germany to attain expansion, world-power, a "place in the sun" was by defeating England. Hence the tension between England and Germany was growing and the race in European armaments came to mean primarily competition in the building of warships. The coming fight for the dominion over the Old World was expected to take place on sea. All that has now suddenly changed, and that change has come as an after-effect of the Balkan Wars.

Germany had hitherto been facing chiefly West. She has no quarrel with Russia. The interests of these two countries nowhere collide; on the contrary, there is much which binds Berlin and St. Petersburg with close ties to each other. Berlin is not truly German, just as St. Petersburg is not Russian. The real national capital of German life and culture would have to lie somewhere on the Main or Rhine, the true Russian centre would have to be found in Moscow or somewhere on the Volga. Berlin and St. Petersburg are military camps, artificially raised into capitals and great cities. Both lie in the same geographical sphere, in the region of the same culture. Both of them are seats of the Baltic gentry; the Pomeranian "Junkers" are cousins of the Livonian nobility, and this not merely in the metaphorical sense. The Russian Government is run by an aristocracy of Baltic

Germans and by a German bureaucracy which are united by tradition, and often even by ties of blood, to the class that rules in Berlin. Their ideals are identical. The Russian Chancellor, Nesselrode, a German who stood at the head of the Russian Government for more than forty years, but never managed to learn to speak the Russian language well, warned his successors to adhere faithfully to the Prussian friendship; for both States have a common interest in sustaining autocratic government and their common anti-Polish policy.

Thus, as long as the Government of Russia is run in accordance with the principles of the St. Petersburg bureaucracy, no danger threatens Germany from that side. But how long will it be possible for the Russian Germans and their allies to preserve the upper hand? Since the days of Frederick II there never has been a great Russian statesman or general who did not make use and take advantage of, but who at the same time did not fear, the immeasurable, hidden forces of the Russian Empire and the incalculable, deep, mystical spirit of the Russian people. Russia is ruled by the Russian Germans, and still the people hate them. They have no place in the cultural life of the country; they remain strangers. They have no understanding for, and still less sympathy with, the Russian Nationalist, Pan-Slav movement; that movement naturally turns against the Germans within and without the Russian Empire. A mighty wave of Pan-Slav feeling may some day sweep away the German Government from St. Petersburg and put an end to their influence on Russian foreign policy. The Balkan War and the crisis in Austro-Russian relations, which was caused thereby, have proved an enormous stimulus to Nationalist feeling in Russia.

If the Russian Government, owing to a further growth of that feeling, became imbued with the Pan-Slav spirit and made Pan-Slav aims the basis of its foreign policy, this change, with whatever potential dangers it might threaten Germany in the future, would not in any way immediately imperil her position in Europe, were it not for her connexion with Austria-Hungary. The alliance of these two governments is, perhaps, the firmest of all European alliances. Without the sheltering help of Germany, Austria could not survive long. On the other hand, a disruption of the Austrian State would imply the greatest set-back which German influence in Europe could possibly meet with.

For purposes of foreign policy Austria as a country is a dead body, without any inherent force or initiative of its own. In that extraordinary conglomeration of nationalities, each of which pursues its own, divergent aims, no resultant of public opinion can ever be formed. That which is most ardently wished for by one part of the country is equally dreaded by some other section. The outcome is a total paralysis of what people imagine to be " public opinion," in so far as the foreign policy of the State is concerned. Owing to the neutralising influence which the different groups exercise on one another, any government in Vienna, even if purely bureaucratic in its character, has a free hand in the direction of foreign policy, and as a matter of fact the Vienna Foreign Office is not in any way dependent on the Austrian Parliament, though it has to reckon with the Hungarian Diet. The ultimate deciding factor in Austro-Hungarian foreign policy, however, is the *Hofburg* (the Court). As the Imperial Government sees in Germany its only reliable ally and its only safeguard against disruption, the Habsburg Monarchy has become, in European politics, a mere appendix to Germany. Thus, through its inert, but still cohering body, the influence of Berlin now reaches far down to the south and east of Europe, and, moreover, Germany can count on the support of the Austro-Hungarian army which, however bad the political conditions in the country are, remains one of the best in Europe. Were Austria to dissolve, German influence would be thrown back beyond the Czech lands, Vienna would change into one of the furthest German outposts to the south-east, and Germany would find herself shut off from the Adriatic Sea, and therefore also from the Mediterranean, by an impenetrable Italian and South-Slavonic wall. She could exercise no more direct influence in Balkan affairs than, for example, Italy can in those of Belgium or Holland. Through a disruption of Austria, Germany would be practically changed from a Central-European into a merely North-European power.

As was stated above, with Germany Russia has no quarrel, nor does she particularly desire to acquire any of her territory. Her position is very different in regard to Austria; Russia aims in no ambiguous way at the acquisition of Galicia, and favours the Great-Serbian movement in the south. The " coming dissolution of Austria " has by now become a current topic of political discussion in Russia, just as " the sick man of Turkey " had been during the preceding two centuries.

The danger which threatens Austria from Russia is still more emphasised by the changes which the recent wars have produced in the Balkan Peninsula. Up to 1911, Austria and Germany, in their Balkan policy, relied upon the support of, and in turn supported, Turkey and Roumania against their Slav neighbours, Bulgaria, Serbia and Montenegro, while Russia favoured the latter. When the First Balkan War had practically annihilated Turkey as an European power, a re-shuffling of alliances followed. In that re-shuffling Austria came to back the wrong horse; led by her anti-Serbian bias, she favoured the formation of the Albanian State and fastened on Bulgaria as the coming dominant power in the Peninsula. She encouraged Bulgaria in the adventurous policy of the Second Balkan War, with a consequent loss of territory, power and prestige to Bulgaria. At the same time, by supporting her, Austria found herself in opposition to Roumania. As a matter of fact, now that Russian acquisitions in the Balkans have become utterly impossible, and that Serbia and not Bulgaria has become Russia's ward and ally, an anti-Austrian policy is much more natural for Roumania than an Austrian alliance. If a territory inhabited by a few hundred thousand Roumanians remains in the hands of Russia, the number of Roumanians inhabiting Austria and Hungary amounts to a few millions; an aggrandisement of Roumania by the acquisition of the Roumanian parts of Transylvania and the Bukovina is much more feasible than by the recovery of Western Bessarabia. Roumanian national interests are therefore quite likely to force her King, a Hohenzollern, into a Russian alliance.

The net result of the Balkan Wars for Austria is the loss of her ally Turkey, an increase in the power of her enemy, Serbia (which is strengthened by an alliance and community of interests with Greece), and the estrangement of Roumania. Bulgaria will venture on no new enterprises under Austrian leadership, while Albania is more likely to become a source of weakness to the Triple Alliance, by giving rise to friction between Italy and Austria, than to be of any positive use to it in the diplomatic and military game. Thus before 1911 the Balkan Peninsula was, owing to the divergent interests of the different States, balanced within itself; now it presents a definitely anti-Austrian array.

The southern frontier of Austria requires then more defence than it ever had need of before; and meantime in the north, Russia is arming on an enormous scale. Hence Austria-Hungary must do the same, and so must Germany, having so much at stake in the safety of Austria.

"Concentration" on the European Continent has become the new watchword in Germany. It is no use starting quarrels about some swamps in the Congo or some rocks in Morocco when problems of so much greater weight and of so much more pressing urgency threaten nearer at home. German trade and shipping will develop as they have hitherto, and no one thinks of attacking them in any way. But the aggressive, political side of the German *Weltpolitik* has disappeared. Germany is now far too much occupied with affairs in Eastern Europe to contemplate any move against England. England, as the Power barring the way to expeditions of which the Germans have ceased to think, no longer evokes any anger in Germany; and in England a certain sense of relief is felt at present after the acute tension of recent years. The expense required for armaments on land against Russia is so heavy that it has become very doutbful whether Germany and Austria will be able to continue, and still more doubtful whether they will be able, to increase in the future their naval programmes.

GERMANS AND RUSSIA

(" *Land and Water,*" *April* 13*th,* 1916)

For centuries they have been watching the calm, white face of a silent god, they have gazed at the patient, mute eyes of a suffering people. They have cursed it, and they have taught it; they have feared it, and they have bullied it; they tried to wring from it and master the unknown, they tried to bring it to the level of their own thinking, to conquer it, to transform it and to destroy it. It remained. Then it became a nightmare to them. Sometimes Germans describe it as the spirit of the Russian soil, as the spirit of the Russian people. The " spirit of a people," what is it? Merely a phrase, a subterfuge of those who in self-defence try to enclose life into abstract words and meaningless descriptions, so that they may master it, measure it and juggle with it at pleasure.

Go into the endless sad plains of Russia, among her infinitely patient peasant folk. What can you Germans do with them? For you always wish to do something. You and your work and your thoughts will pass over Russia as the wind that straggles across the plains. Even in that wind there is more than in your wisdom; it is part of infinite Nature. It has wandered across the steppes, it has seen the rising sun, the cornfields have bowed to it, and it has talked to the trees in the forests, and it goes on towards an endless, unknown future; like the Russian people. Men have listened to its songs, to the songs which it sings to lonely men in the wide, open fields, and it has listened to the mute sighs of patient, suffering men, who work silently, waiting for the day whose coming none can tell. But what are your thoughts—what are those artificial, stillborn creatures which you call ideas? "Children of the Spirit?" What is the spirit which is not man, which neither suffers nor rejoices, but merely prides itself on an unreal existence? Your ideas will pass away unheeded.

You call the Eastern man aggressive because he is not willing to fight you on your own level. Why should he fight against you? You are the "dumb ones,"[1] the strangers who come and go. The Russian peasant can put up with much that is unpleasant, and Russia has put up with plenty of Germans. Why have you so suddenly grown fierce? What do you fear, you clever, efficient, victorious people? You have been insulted; Russian life itself is an insult to you. You tried

[1] Germans are called in Slav languages by a word which signifies "the dumb men"; "Slavs" are the "worded ones."

to transform it and you failed; you tried to understand it and you shuddered; you tried to deny it in a wild, hysterical cry, and the same silent, patient eyes still look at you with amazement. Poor amazing German folk! You do not even know how to suffer. Your conceit is too great, your achievements are too magnificent, your philosophy is too highly developed. You have asked Russian life for its *philosophische, erkenntnisstheoretische Errungenschaften*,[1] and you got no answer; so you called the Russians barbarians. Then why do you fear them? And, by God, you do fear them.

There was a German poet who wrote delicate lyrics, that skim the æsthetic surface of the life of the educated rich. He has also written several novels which describe the sordid German *Nachtleben*. The writer's name was Otto Julius Bierbaum. He was very *deutsch*, and in the year 1912 set out to study *das Phänomenon Dostojewski*. He has come very near being tragic. He escaped it by a hairbreadth. He saw a strange god, and did not strive with him. He shut his eyes and did not dare to keep them shut; and he finished by playing hide-and-seek like a little child, he, the great spokesman of a *Kultur-Nation*. He did not dare to keep his eyes shut, for he suffered from an *europäisches Kulturgewissen* (a European con-

[1] "Achievements in the philosophical theory of knowledge."

science for culture), and he did not care to keep them open, for he felt that he was shaken in his conceit as he gazed at the calm, open features of the man who had the courage to see, because he had neither the desire to judge nor the impulse to change the things which he saw.

The German writer feels that "a kind of perversion of his natural feelings overcomes him," his pride on which he prides himself is in danger of vanishing before the suffering, the understanding and the crushing humility of that simple human giant Dostoyevsky. Bierbaum wishes for a Nietzschean "transvaluation of all values," but values must remain; there must be definite values, otherwise how could there be pride of achievement?

"Dostoyevsky is truly great," says Bierbaum, "though at bottom I don't like him : he oppresses me more often than he uplifts me. I know it now, he is not a peak, he is a mountain system. All our modern peaks, excepting only one, reach scarcely to half the height of his middle chain. The one who excels his height is Nietzsche; but beside the enormous massif of live-rock, that peak looks to a terrifying degree like a work of art, like something made, beside things elemental." Nietzsche's ideal expressed itself at its best in one giant statue, in his superman Zarathustra. Dostoyevsky has created crowds of men; none of them takes thought to add to his own stature, they bow to the ground in the sad, humble consciousness of their human lives. And yet, when looking from a distance at his living crowd, one perceives " a colossal figure resembling the images of those Indian gods with hundreds of heads, with thousands of arms, uniting in their bodies all the generations: the giant people of Russia."

Moments come when the German feels that he can no longer stand up as judge, as a wise and cultured judge, against the poor, great man Dostoyevsky. He follows him as in the old legend the children followed the mystic piper. He looks to him as to a saint, he would adore him, and pray to him for miracles. " His works are . . . self-crucifixion; all literary confessions vanish before the stations of his Cross, there is no word which could express the adoration . . . when one sees that suffering man rise up again and again on his path toward Calvary; he loves the pain, and with the pain he loves humanity. . . . But without any pathos, without any pose. One might think of the images of the Byzantine Christ. But only for a moment. For the magnificence of Byzantium is lacking. Dostoyevsky is the very opposite of a *schöne Seele* (a beautiful soul). He was too great for that."

Dostoyevsky understood the heart of man and knew the name of God. He loved that which the world despises and crushes in contempt, says Bierbaum, but "which internally is glorious and sublime." And his love for it was not that of mercy, not even that of compassion; he wanted to change nothing, for he knew the secret glory which lives in debasement and suffering, and rejoiced in it. Before Dmitri Fyodorovitch, the brazen, animal, and yet so passionately human Karamazoff, Father Zosima fell to the ground in silent, feeling reverence; and he sent his disciple Alyosha into the world to live man's life, to learn the mystery of good and evil, and the meaning of things which lie beyond the realm of either. It is beyond their borders that reveals itself the true sense of existence, for redemption cannot be of this world, material achievements are froth, and freedom and power are to be found only in feeling and understanding.

Is that, then, his Gospel? "If so, we have arrived at a point where the instinct of the man of Western Culture refuses to follow any further the sorcerer Dostoyevsky." He refuses to work miracles? He is not "a saint of action"? He will not use his power to any material purpose? He cannot therefore crush us. Our simple and sane German mind and German wisdom are stronger than he! The charm is broken; a broad, greasy grin spreads over the fat, angular face of the German writer. "*Na, ja, Verehrtester*, at the best we may use you as an interesting exhibit!" It was only when dazed by fear that the eyes of the German had seen the glories of things which lie beyond the reach of calculation. The mystic piper has left the land of dreams, the golden stars of his magic robes have died away, his power has vanished. The German brings him back as captive into the land of values; he is now hardly anything but an interesting fool— the disciple has changed into his impresario. He will explain *das Phänomenon Dostojewski* and charge an entrance fee. The German nation is safe. It has no reason to fear; it will make profits from trading in Russian " spiritual values," as for centuries it has by trading with the bodies, property and freedom of the Russian nation. Heroes when it is safe, otherwise hucksters.

" Sincerely prepared to admire those virtuosi of humility as extraordinary men," says Bierbaum, " and to ascribe to them powers akin to those of saints, we refuse to accept them as examples and models for humanity at large. . . . And we enjoy the confident hope that, if the Russian spirit is really affected by this inclination towards passivity, which we consider sublime but yet diseased, then there is no danger of our being overwhelmed by it. Processions of flagellants do not conquer the world. . . ."

" That which has made Dostoyevsky so great is

perhaps just the thing which will prevent the Russian nation from becoming great as against ourselves. But even assuming that this spirit answers the Russian heart, and is therefore beneficial to it, it can hardly further our own development. For it seems that we are not made to enter into it in the way shown to us by that, after all for us very strange, phenomenon Dostoyevsky. To follow his spirit would mean to deny Goethe and to consider Nietzsche a disease. . . ."

The Germans will never do that; but Goethe did not care for Germany, and Nietzsche prided himself on his foreign, Slav extraction.

TROTSKY

(" *The New Europe*," *January* 17th, 1918)

Leo Braunstein, better known as Trotsky, was born in Odessa some forty years ago of a Jewish family. Because of his name and the embarrassment which he has caused to Great Britain, he is currently reported in this country to be a German Jew, who found it convenient to hide his identity under an assumed Russian name. His original name really proves that his family did not come from Germany, and the new name was meant to disguise his person, not his race or extraction.

Braunstein is one of those innumerable names, compounded of German, common to Jews in Eastern Europe. At the time when Poland was partitioned, most Polish Jews had no family names, but were simply known by their personal names and patronymics—as Abraham, son of Moses, or Isaac, son of Solomon. The Prussian and Austrian officials, who in 1795 obtained dominion over what subsequently became Russian Poland, manufactured names by the thousand for the Jews, going through the whole gamut of flowers, animals, colours and stones, sometimes venturing, to the best of their German taste, upon attempts at humour. If a Jew's name is Offenbach or Hildesheimer or Speyer, one may assume that his family has come from one of the Rhenish towns, but if it is Blumenduft (scent of flowers) or Unterleibsgeschwür (abdominal ulcer—an authentic case!), it is clear that an ancestor of his was the object of German mockery, or of subsequent Russian imitation. If such a man goes to Germany, his name will immediately stamp him to the true Teuton as an East-European Hebrew, and he has to travel all the way to England before he is conceded the status of a full-blown German or of a German Jew.

Braunstein-Trotsky had no reason to hide his race, which was a matter of complete indifference to the Socialists among whom he has spent his life. Names for special use in party activities, the so-called " party names," were assumed by Jewish and Gentile revolutionaries alike, and the tale which they tell is of the years which, for the sake of an ideal, these men have spent without a home and without a real name—hunted beasts, hiding their identities from the most highly-organised secret police in the world. When Leo Braunstein chose his " party name " he naturally did not feel bound to imitate the humour or the scientific methods of the German officials who had labelled his ancestors; yet the name Trotsky still suggests a Jewish origin to the average Russian, for it is derived from the town of Troki, in the very heart of the old Jewish Pale.

When a student of the Juridical Faculty at Odessa, Trotsky joined the Socialist movement. Some revolutionary *fracas* or conspiracy led to his expulsion from the University and started him on his career of Socialist propaganda, diversified by years in Siberia and in prison. The men of the Russian Revolution are now frequently described in Western Europe as " wind-bags " or " talkers " by people who have never known Russian prisons or Siberia. Let them read the gruesome story of Maria Spiridonova, which at one time made the whole civilised world shudder (the recent Peasants' Congress at Petrograd elected Maria Spiridonova its president). Or let them read Leo Deutsch's " Reminiscences of Siberia," or any other lives from that new martyrology. There has been horror in the past experience of these men and women: a madness has been engendered by it and a fanaticism which alone has enabled them to endure all things and conquer in the end.

In Trotsky the fanatic is much less conspicuous than in most Bolshevik leaders. Socialism supplies him with an outlook rather than with doctrines. He is clear-sighted, he understands the logic of events, the force of ideas, their uncompromising nature, and the need for simplicity and cogency in political thinking. Where minor men are unbending from pedantry, experience forbids Trotsky to compromise in matters of principle. He knows the only terms on which one can fight with the arms of the spirit against material weapons, and he knows how to capture the man behind the machine gun, instead of countering the two in their own kind. In 1905 he fought autocracy and succumbed—the Russian army had remained with the Tsar: twelve years later it went over to the Revolution. In July 1917 he fought Kerensky and succumbed: the army was with his rival. In November he won without having raised or armed new forces. He is now [January 1918] trying the same game on Germany, nay, on the entire world—each man has only one method of acting, just as he has only one face.

Can Trotsky win this time? He will undoubtedly succumb again, but the seed will have been sown. That quaint idea of "the dictatorship of the proletariat" will remain, a burning sign to those who have a sense of wrong: it is not democracy which the Bolsheviks aim at, but "a turn of the wheel"—the rule of the downtrodden. They address to the upper classes what Meredith calls "the parent question of humanity: 'Am I thy master or thou mine?'"

If their sign is to endure, if their teachings are to work in the consciousness of the masses, they must remain pure. For ideas compromise with reality means a kind of decay; it may be like the decay of fruit at seed-time; but if the fruit perishes when the seed is still immature, the loss is unredeemed and uncompensated. Conservatism is the philosophy of reality; revolution results from the logic of ideas.

If Trotsky compromises, he is lost; if he does not, he is probably lost too—which few men are likely to regret more than he himself. He is not a calm, iron ascetic with a deeply human heart and an inhuman mind, like Lenin. His *naturel* has proved too strong even for the long schooling of Russian revolutionary life. Trotsky enjoys life, loves pleasure, is very ambitious and rather vain: he cares for Trotsky and thinks a deal of him, so much, indeed, that at moments this foolhardy fighter becomes accessible to doubt and fear. He enjoys power and has a sense of humour, and the humour of power seems to appeal to him almost as much as its responsibility (this also fits him admirably for dealing with European Chanceleries). There is nothing of the pathos about him which attached to Kerensky, the Hamlet of the Russian Revolution. He will make himself respected, men shall reckon with him, the world must not forget Trotsky or leave him out of account. He imposes himself on it by his cleverness and energy. These qualities have served him well with crowds and with women. To vain men no one can replace success on the wider stage so well as women; they are the perfect audience for " Kings in Babylon."

Trotsky has been poor all his life. He has lived in garrets, has starved, and yet has thought of how the world should be ruled. He knows what life is to those cast into the outer darkness. Easeful pleasure is suited for men who safely possess; destruction is the instinct, the living art and the wild joy of the dispossessed—the dark, cynical, defiant face of Michael Angelo's statue of Brutus menaces the exquisite and aristocratic beauty of Leonardo da Vinci. As Trotsky has been poor all his life, the usual stories are now told of his having been bribed by the Germans. " German agent " is the most appropriate label for anyone who does not suit us. The curse of being a politician and poor is temptation, and next, that even if the man resists temptation, there is circumstantial evidence to suggest the opposite. The only temptation which approaches the rich politician and to which he duly succumbs is that of giving bribes—he " nurses " his constituency, subscribes to party funds, ends by buying hereditary legislative power in the House of Lords, and remains " respectable—damned respectable."

TROTSKY

Trotsky achieved prominence for the first time during the revolution of 1905. Nosar ("party name" : Hrustalev), an insignificant person, was chairman of the Central Soviet. Trotsky, his assistant, supplied the brains of the movement, and it was with him that the Prime Minister, Count Witte, negotiated previous to the publication of the October Manifesto. After the collapse of the revolution, Trotsky sought refuge abroad and relapsed into comparative obscurity. Unequalled as an agitator, a speaker, a man of action, Trotsky is not the leader for a persecuted creed, who could fortify them in their devout prayers in the Catacombs, or—to give the Russian-Socialist equivalent—take part with all seriousness in their sterile discussions in exile. Trotsky's Socialism is sincere, his very temperament is revolutionary Socialism, he is carried away by it. He thinks through his temperament. In the white heat of abstract passion he sees issues with a logical consistency such as cannot be attained in the every-day perception of reality, when comparatively small accidents of environment compete with the ideas which are the work of the speculative human understanding. To Trotsky Socialism and its creed have become his world, and he could hardly live or act outside their sphere. But the theoretical differences between the various Socialist groups were unessential to him at a time when as yet none of their doctrines could give rise to action. His restless ambition, his excitable temper, his desire for action, made him shift from one Socialist group to another, while blind zeal and lack of humour made other men persevere and attain leadership. Trotsky finished by being called " the morass " by those strong in faith—the uncertain, dangerous ground between the immovable mountains.

August 1914 found him in Paris. His first move was an attack on the German Socialists for having voted war-credits. During the next two years he edited a Russian Socialist paper. Towards the end of 1916 the French Government, to disembarrass itself of Trotsky, decided to put him across the Swiss frontier; it seemed that there he would remain high and dry till the end of the war. He succeeded, however, in getting himself sent to Spain instead, and thence embarked for America. To one born in bondage, chained in his youth, exiled in his manhood, the Revolution of 1917 was the sign that the days of sterile misery had come to an end. Not yet! By order of the British authorities Trotsky was forcibly taken off a homeward-bound Norwegian steamer and interned at Halifax. Those few weeks of detention in Nova Scotia did not kill him; but, as Machiavelli, puts it—*si vendicano gli uomini delle leggiere offese ; delle gravi non possono.* The remembrance of wrong done to his own person rendered more pointed Trotsky's action for the release of Chicherin. Yet the first document compromising to the German Government which he selected for publication was a letter from the Kaiser to the Tsar, complaining of the asylum accorded to revolutionaries in Great Britain, and proposing joint representations on that subject. Trotsky thus reminded his comrades of the time when Prussia had offered itself as an assistant to their hangmen, and Prince Bülow sneered at "Silberfarb" and "Mandelstamm"! Not even our most God-forsaken official underlings with a *flair* for the psychological moment when petty chicanery creates the maximum of irritation can altogether wipe out the memory of those other days.

The pre-revolutionary opposition in the Duma was political; the revolution which broke out in the streets, social. The Cadets [1] aimed at constitutional reform and at a more efficient prosecution of the war. They could not give the sign for active revolt, lest it should interfere with the conduct of the war. The revolution was made by men to whom the war was not the first concern. The Cadets joined it after the day was won. The peasantry and army cried out for land and peace.

---

[1] "Cadets" was the abbreviation for Constitutional Democrats, the Russian Liberals of those days.

The Cadets desired to go on with the war till victory was won, and to check social revolution. These were two irreconcilable programmes. Kerensky tried to reconcile them. He wanted all classes to unite, to offer sacrifices and to have confidence in each other. The masses were to submit to the leadership and discipline of the educated *bourgeoisie*, suffer yet further in a war of which they hardly understood the meaning, and trust to the upper classes not to use in future their regained power for preventing the social revolution. The upper classes were to work cheerfully, viewing with equanimity the certain doom in store for them on the conclusion of peace. Kerensky's endeavours were met with opposition, nay, with direct *sabotage*, from the Right and the Left, and with scant understanding among the Western Allies. His attempt broke down.

Then came Trotsky's day and burden. With him and the Bolsheviks the strangest factor has entered the war—a belligerent power to whom war on national lines has neither sense nor meaning. The only war which they understand is between classes, and that war knows no frontiers. It is not peace which they carry to the world, but strife; they are militants, but in a different dimension. Could Trotsky raise, arm and officer a sufficiently big army he would menace, not the Central Powers alone, but all the *bourgeois* Governments of the world; though he would probably try to avoid fighting their armies in battles which indiscriminately sacrifice *bourgeois* and proletarians. He naturally demands complete self-determination for all nationalities throughout the world—which implies, among other things, the end of German imperialism, the complete disruption of the Habsburg Monarchy and of the Turkish Empire (one has to come to England to find Socialists or " democrats " who, from sheer controversial perversity, become champions of such dynastic creations !). But to Trotsky self-determination is merely one aspect of a much wider problem. " Why should people object so strongly to the dominion of one nation over another," the Bolshevik would say, " and yet within the same nation admit that one man should be born in economic subjection to another man ? Why talk about ' submerged nationalities ' and be silent about submerged classes ? " To the Bolsheviks the different ideas of possession and dominion are but parts of one organic whole of which the vital nerve may be destroyed by a violent blow, but which it is almost impossible to transform by degrees. Evolution comes after revolution to eliminate the moribund forms by a gradual process. That is why systems survive revolutions, and yet cannot be killed apart from revolution. As Hartmann put it in 1848, referring to the constitutional problem raised by the French Revolution—

> "Das ist der Zeiten bittere Not,
> Der Widerspruch der schwer zu heben,
> Dass die Monarchie wohl tot,
> Aber die Monarchen leben."

Most of Trotsky's ideas are incomprehensible to the illiterate masses in the armies and peasantry of Russia which have raised him to power. They want peace because they are tired of fighting, not because they hold any particular views on international relations. They desire to expropriate the rich without any clear idea of the condition which is to supplant the order they destroy. The immense, almost inconceivable, suffering inflicted on the Russian peasant-soldier during the first three years of the war by the criminal callousness and corruption of the *ancien régime* has resulted in a psychological catastrophe—a disappearance of military and social discipline unequalled in history, and a collapse of routine and tradition, the framework of everyday life. The intellectual revolutionaries sail in the storm, and their sails rise over the waves, in appearance a triumphant sign of the storm itself. Yet they have no real control over the blind elemental forces which cannot be disciplined, least of all by the revolutionaries themselves. For if Trotsky tried to coerce them and succeeded in that attempt—which in reality is impossible—he would break the very spirit and force of the revolution. He is not the man for such work.

Without an army at his command, with a country plunged in anarchy and demanding peace, with masses only very dimly comprehending the meaning of the events which now unfold, Trotsky has to face the Teutonic Powers [January 1918]. It would seem that he is at their mercy. And yet a dark fear haunts his opponents. There is the suffering and despair of their own peoples, their craving for peace, their rage, which, hitherto silent, may any moment burst out in a desperate cry. They, too, have heard the watchword about " the rule of the downtrodden " and " the turn of the wheel." It is to them that Trotsky speaks over the heads of their rulers. What do the starving German masses care for dominion over other races? Has not enough blood been shed? Are the maimed and crippled too few in number? Trotsky speaks sincerely about peace. Russia sets all her nations free. She threatens nobody. If peace negotiations break down, will anyone believe that it was through Russia's fault? German and Austrian statesmen wriggle, they manœuvre for positions; they make the most amazing professions of principle and contradict them in the same breath, they try to set themselves right in the eyes of their peoples. Trotsky unmasks their game and analyses aloud each move they make. The scene is almost grotesque. As Dr. Harold Williams put it in one of his Petrograd despatches, the Germans " are in the position of the mediæval knight, playing a weird game of chess with supernatural powers."

If the war continues, what can the German Government do? Can it risk ordering its armies across the undefended Russian front? Will they obey? Will they attack the country which was the first to offer peace? Perhaps. But if the Germans get to Russia—again, what can they do? They cannot coerce Russia. Revolutionary Russia is already a nightmare to them, and even from their own country Germany's rulers cannot eliminate any more the forces and ideas which the war has set in motion.

METTERNICH'S DOCTRINE [1]

("The Times Literary Supplement," January 28th, 1926)

A HEGELIAN once described the Napoleonic period as the sixth day of Creation, for a man had arisen; it was followed by the Sabbath Day of history when all creative power seemed at rest. A cold shadow lay over Europe for thirty-three years, the active life of a generation, and people connected it with the person of Metternich and called it his "system," though they never ceased to wonder how that rococo figure in porcelain, stylish and nimble, and in appearance hollow and brittle, could last so long and keep off the light from tens of millions of men. In his youth described as "*le ministre-papillon*," in his old age as a blind, senseless fossil, he was none the less credited with the power to stop the stars in their courses. It is this incongruity between Metternich's personality and his reputed achievements that constitutes the seeming enigma.

He himself denied having devised any "system" —it was "*eine Weltordnung*" ("a world order"),

---

[1] "Metternich." By Heinrich Ritter von Srbik. Two volumes. (Munich: F. Bruckmann. 48s.)

based on deep immutable laws which his own clear spirit had merely discerned and laid bare to the eyes of men. The aristocrat and the diplomat, the professor and the prophet, and finally the old actor and buffoon, were quaintly blended in the person of Metternich when, in discourses and despatches of ever-growing length, year after year, he propounded his doctrines to a world over which his master-mind seemed to preside. But the more he talked and wrote, the less apparent were the positive contents of his teaching, till people began to doubt whether there were any. The mistake was in accepting the would-be philosophic and scientific character which Metternich gave to his harangues; these were songs, in which the music mattered and not the text.

Conservatism, of which Metternich was an exponent, is primarily based on a proper recognition of human limitations, and cannot be argued in a spirit of self-glorifying logic. The history of the French Revolution and of Napoleon had shown once more the immense superiority which existing social forms have over human movements and genius, and the poise and rest which there are in a spiritual inheritance, far superior to the thoughts, will or inventions of any single generation. It was the greatness and strength of Metternich during these fateful years to have foreseen that human contrivances, however clever

METTERNICH'S DOCTRINE

and beneficial, would not endure, and to have understood the peculiar elasticity with which men would finally revert to former habits. The failure of striving, struggling men brings the heir of ages back into his own. The fine and, in its own way, unique diplomacy of Metternich, during both the Napoleonic era and the years which followed, was based on this deep, almost instinctive, understanding of Conservatism. He annotated the margins of the great book of human insufficiency and inertia—interesting work indeed, which requires a strong and free mind, but which ought to be undertaken in a spirit of humility. Of this there is no trace in Metternich. He was essentially of the eighteenth century, a disciple of Voltaire rather than of Rousseau. He shared its belief in the infinite power of the human mind (exemplified to him in his own person), though not in the unlimited perfectibility of human nature; much interested in science, he liked to treat of society and politics in terms of immutable, abstract laws, and, unaware of the inadequacy of the data we possess, allowed a sterile, doctrinaire logic to repress psychological perception. His scientific interests themselves had the typical eighteenth-century turn towards things curious and extraordinary rather than towards the basic average, and mainly served to supply him with a pseudo-scientific jargon and with what a bitter critic once called his " five metaphors." He was sentimental, but disliked melodrama; he professed feelings, but shrank from enthusiasms; he could loathe, but not hate. He remained classic in an age of romantics, and worshipped reason, but denied creative power to human thought. He, for one, certainly lacked it; he was a *raisonneur* rather than a thinker—"*Je raisonne sur tout et en toute occasion.*"

Like the eighteenth century, he knew States and not nations. He abhorred the idea of the sovereignty of the people and failed to see that, after all, it was just an abstract idea, incapable of full realisation, and therefore doomed to compromises. It has been alleged that his ideas were based on the needs and calculated to serve the peculiar interests of Austria; but it is hardly in the power of man successfully to develop *ad hoc* systems. Metternich was sincerely attached to the Habsburg Monarchy because, like no other State, it was bound up with the time and world in which he would have chosen to live, and because its very existence was a denial of nationality and popular sovereignty; he rose to the first place in it because his ideas so completely answered its needs and nature. He was not an Austrian by birth, but from the Rhine, and he was twenty-one when he first came to Vienna. In fact, he was a Rhenish *émigré*, with the intellectual outlook of the French *ancien régime*; but, not being a Frenchman, was even less capable than the average French aristocrat of sharing in the national developments of revolutionary and Napoleonic France. These antecedents, coupled with the world-wide interests of his class and the non-national character of Austria, made him a true European. " *C'est que depuis longtemps l'Europe a pris pour moi la valeur d'une patrie,*" he declared in 1824 to the Duke of Wellington. With revolution lurking everywhere, he preached international comity to princes and favoured treaties of mutual guarantee for the existing frontiers, which to him, who knew no rights of nationality, presented no other moral problems than those of a private estate. He insisted on the full sovereignty and independence of every State, however small, but as the balance of power required the centre of Europe to be strengthened against France and Russia, he sought to establish the Germanic Confederation, and even dallied with the idea of a *Lega Italica*, paradoxically conceiving both as mere groups of States. Precluded from appealing to the national consciousness of the Germans or Italians, which alone could have supplied the proper basis for such unions and imposed them on recalcitrant princelings, he naturally and necessarily failed in his attempts.

His face was to the West, and yet it was at the

Congress of Vienna that the exclusion of Austria from West-Central Europe was begun. Prussia, which in 1789 had stood practically outside Germany, tucked away in the north-eastern corner, now acquired the Rhineland; while Austria, deprived of Belgium and the Breisgau, gained in internal coherence but lost all foothold and immediate interest in Western Germany. Clearly the Power which held 'the Watch on the Rhine' was bound ultimately to lead Germany. Neither Metternich nor the Prussian statesmen had planned this change or fully foreseen its consequences, and it was wrong to explain it by a wish on his part to withdraw Austria from direct contact with France; possibilities of conflict between them remained in Italy, and Metternich, the Rhinelander, was the last man to wish for a withdrawal from the West.

Strictly speaking, Metternich was not the reactionary he is usually represented; for this he was too intelligent, too cautious and too conservative. He honoured all prescriptive rights and vested interests. For him the British Parliamentary system was proper in its own home, but not a panacea for nations which had not developed it. Within the Habsburg Monarchy itself he tolerated and protected Hungary's old constitution, based though it was on a Parliament; it was not for him to destroy the growth of many centuries. But he seemed unable to conceive how anything new could ever be safely attempted without leading to the collapse of the entire social fabric; his own logic was too rigid and destructive. Theoretically he argued that stability was not synonymous with immobility; but in practice he loathed even the change of years, having by December become attached to the four figures of the date. Metternich was not an administrator, and did not claim to be one; he lacked the necessary energy, perseverance and mastery of practical detail. But he cannot truly be held responsible for the administrative chaos and decay of Austria during the years of his Chancellorship. He merely enabled her to exist so long being what she was; though it was no accident that he was riveted to such a State, as his fundamental ideas excluded the new elements of national life. Nor can he be blamed for Austria's intellectual backwardness; with him or without him Vienna has never produced anything truly great or creative, only a fine blend of a peculiar internationalism with an intensely local colouring —something like Metternich himself.

The real strength and dignity of his nature revealed itself in the days of his fall and the years of his retirement. "*Eh bien, est-ce que nous sommes tous morts ?*" asked his wife as he returned from the Imperial Palace after the revolution in the streets of Vienna had forced his resignation. "*Oui, ma chère, nous sommes morts.*" Unmoved and unshaken, he accepted his moral death. But when on the steps of the British Museum he met another great exile, Guizot, he remarked with a smile: "*L'erreur n'a jamais approché de mon esprit.*"

Almost seventy years have passed since his death, and no satisfactory biography has appeared; and now Herr von Srbik's work, monumental as it is in size, fullness of detail and erudition, might with some justice be called an encyclopædia rather than a biography. Even as such it is highly welcome, and will prove of the greatest use to any student of the period. But to read it from beginning to end is indeed a vast undertaking; it consists of two volumes containing 1260 large pages of text, besides 146 pages of footnotes collected at the end. Herr von Srbik has done all he could to make his work complete, but perhaps not enough to render it readable. It is heavy as clay, lifeless and unmoulded.

THE AUSTRIAN REVOLUTION [1]

("*The Times Literary Supplement*," *August 30th, 1923*)

ACTIVE statesmen seldom write contemporary history. One gathers it mostly from the memoirs of " ex-men " who, with their own achievements and hopes engulfed in disaster, publish apologias, often of very considerable historical value, but usually overcast by the deadening shadow of irretrievable defeat and distorted by personal grievances and regrets. Here, however, is a book of a very different kind, the history of a mass movement by the man who, as events have proved, has best understood its nature and setting. Now that the movement has reached a critical point, he sets to work to trace for his companions the course they have gone, to interpret developments which it was beyond their power to control, and to define their present position. The book serves a practical purpose; but the concise and brilliant survey it gives, especially of the years 1914 to 1920, written with thorough knowledge, insight and impartiality, should

[1] " Die oesterreichische Revolution." By Dr. Otto Bauer. (Vienna: Verlag der Wiener Volksbuchhandlung.)

secure for it an important place in historical literature.

The pre-war programme of the Austrian Socialists favoured cultural autonomy on a non-territorial basis as a solution for the racial problems of Austria. Dr. Bauer did not share that view; in an essay published in 1905 he asserted that cultural autonomy within the Habsburg Monarchy could not ultimately satisfy its nationalities. On his return from war imprisonment in Russia, he resumed, at the head of the left wing of the Austrian-German Socialists, his opposition to the Austrian phantasies of the older leaders—*e.g.* to the pseudo-Socialist sophistries of Dr. Renner (later on first Chancellor of the Austrian Republic), who professed to see in the mediæval, dynastic Habsburg Monarchy the "supernational" State of the future, an organisation much superior to the national, "*bourgeois*" creations of the nineteenth century. On November 12th, 1918, Dr. Bauer became Foreign Secretary of the German-Austrian Republic, and, in the Coalition Cabinet of March 1919, also President of the Socialisation Commission. He resigned both posts in the summer of 1919, not meaning to press his ideas when rendered impracticable by circumstances, nor to continue in office when unable to realise them; but, even so, he remained the political and intellectual leader of the

Austrian Socialists. His book is therefore to a certain extent autobiographical, but is so in an unobtrusive way.

About 1848 the nationalities inside the Habsburg Monarchy formed two marked strata: there were the historic nations—the Germans, Magyars, Italians and Poles—with well-developed upper classes, and therefore with cultural continuity and an articulate political life; and the peasant races—the Czechs, Slovaks, Yugo-Slavs, Ukrainians and Roumanians—who, having in previous centuries lost their upper classes, had practically no historic existence. But with the rise of a new middle-class intelligentsia and the entry of the working classes into political life, the subject races recovered conscious national individuality and entered upon a bitter struggle against the master nations—and indirectly also against the Habsburgs, who since 1867 had taken the Magyars, Germans and Poles into partnership. The liberation of the subject races in 1918 (incomplete in East Galicia, where the Ukrainians have once more been reduced under Polish dominion) was the much-belated 1789 of East-Central Europe. The introductory chapters of Dr. Bauer's book give a masterly account of the rise of these national movements, of how the war revolutionised them and filled them with the bitterest hostility against the

Habsburgs, of the activities of the Yugo-Slav and Czechoslovak National Committees abroad, and of the Russo-Siberian anabasis of the Czechoslovak legions.

Great-Austrians and Pan-Germans in Austria were united in their war enthusiasms, and at first even the Socialists ranged themselves on the side of the Central Powers ; Tsardom and the danger of a Russian invasion supplied them with a specious excuse. But the victories won over Russia in 1915 merely stiffened the despotic *régime* in Austria.

> " The factories were militarised, the workmen placed under martial law. . . . The Constitution was suspended, Parliament prorogued, the Press muzzled, the civilian population delivered to the bloody assizes of the courts-martial."

A feeling of sullen, repressed hatred was growing among the masses. The murder of the Austrian Premier, Count Stürgkh, by F. Adler in October 1916, and the Russian revolution in March 1917, broke the silence. At Adler's trial it was the Government which stood in the dock. The Austrian authorities were cowed; previously they had hanged thousands of men for trivial reasons, and now they dared not execute the murderer of the Prime Minister. Parliament was convened in May 1917, for the first time during the war.

The fear of revolution, of submerged nationalities and submerged classes, changed the Habsburgs into ardent pacifists. But even while Czernin was negotiating at Brest-Litovsk, in January 1918, a strike broke out in the Austrian munition works and mutinies occurred in the army. The outbreak was premature; sufficient forces were available to quell a revolution, and the leaders had quickly to close this first revolutionary prelude. On January 20th the "Left" of the Austrian Socialists published a statement, partly forecast and partly programme:—

> "The Germans form but a minority in Austria. The predominance of the German bourgeoisie in Austria rests entirely on political and social privileges. Shaken by the economic and cultural rise of the other nationalities, it will break down completely with the victory of democracy. Then the Slav and Latin races of Austria-Hungary will attain Statehood, and from the Austrian conglomerate German Austria will emerge as a separate community . . . free to settle its relations to Germany according to her own needs and will. . . ."

In the union of all Germans in a German Republic, the labour classes of German Austria were to seek their own future.

The events of the next nine months confirmed

Bauer's forecasts. Repressed ideas, set free by the defeat of the Central Powers, moved towards their logical conclusions. By October 30th, 1918, the non-German nationalities had renounced their Habsburg allegiance and a German-Austrian Republic had arisen in fact, though not yet in name, with a Government representing all classes and parties—the expression of a new, revolutionary *contrat social*. The Imperialists still hoped that all this would prove " but a night's intoxication "—if only " the army did not vanish." But, demoralised and defeated, the Austro-Hungarian Army was rolling back on to the hinterland, a wild anarchic horde. The fate of the Habsburg Monarchy was sealed. Even the regiments in garrisons at home dissolved, when more than ever a disciplined armed force was needed. Thereupon the Socialist party, which alone retained a certain hold over the masses, stepped in and, using its own organisations, built up the *Volkswehr* (a popular militia); it thus rendered an important service to the community, but, at the same time, greatly added to its own power and responsibilities.

" Every revolution," writes Dr. Bauer, " has to protect its march against the masses, which, filled with revolutionary illusions and passions, try to conquer more than can be attained or retained under given historic and social conditions." The full advantages of the revolution had to be reaped for the labour classes, and yet they had to be restrained from actions which would have provoked civil war and foreign intervention. The easy victory of a Socialist revolution in and round Vienna would have been answered by the breaking away of the predominantly agrarian provinces and by the stopping of food and coal supplies by the Allied Powers; and its ultimate outcome would have been White Terror, such as Hungary and Bavaria have experienced. These obvious truths the Socialist leaders had to impress on the masses, which were prone to delusions, embittered and brutalised by the war, driven by misery and hunger, elated by the success of the political revolution, incited by the example of Budapest and Munich, and urged on by irresponsible fanatics, foreign agents and artistic intellectuals revelling in revolutionary romantics. The educational task was accomplished in continual practical discussions; every Government measure was discussed with the representatives of the labour organisations, who in turn went into hundreds of meetings to argue, explain and restrain. The party discipline and the authority of the leaders were many a time thrown into the scales; "popularity," said Friedrich Adler, "is an asset for which the only right use is consumption."

Austria is most unfavourably placed for far-reaching social experiments. It is not certain whether, consisting of a few Alpine provinces and the fourth biggest city in Europe (and with the basis on which that city had grown up practically destroyed) she will prove at all capable of the independent existence imposed on her by the Peace Treaties. Anyhow, during the period of readjustment she required the help and the confidence of foreign capital, which could not have been secured had she entered the uncertain road of socialisation. In the way of social reform a great deal was done by the Socialists in the Coalition Governments of 1918 to 1920. But as to ulterior aims, circumstances, experience and, one must add, the good sense of her Socialists, have led Austria on to the safer path of organic development. State management of industries during the war, in all countries alike, has proved how unequal bureaucracies are to the task, while the experience of Russia has shown how little labour stands to gain by violent "expropriations."

> "Democratic socialism [writes Dr. Bauer] is possible only if labour is capable of directing production without destroying it. . . . The rise and development of works committees is therefore of far greater importance for the growth of the Socialist system than

> violent expropriation, if nothing better is to result from it than factories run by a State or a communal bureaucracy."

By working on various committees labour has to prepare for " functional democracy." For this, Dr. Bauer claims, the Austrian revolution and the system evolved by it have laid the foundations, and the change produced " in the mental life of the upper strata among the labour masses is the greatest achievement of the revolution."

Many other subjects are discussed in Dr. Bauer's book: the peace negotiations of St. Germain, Allied policies in East-Central Europe, the growth of the power of labour throughout Europe after the war and its subsequent decline, the financial and economic developments in Austria, the kronen catastrophe and its consequences, the pauperisation of the old middle classes and of the professional intelligentsia, the rise of a new bourgeoisie, etc. The only unsatisfactory chapter is that on the Geneva Agreement and the excellent work done in that matter by the Austrian Chancellor, Dr. Seipel. Dr. Bauer argues that Austria could have been saved by her own resources, without submitting to foreign control. This might have been so, had any Austrian Government had the strength to " axe " its ridiculously overgrown bureaucracy (which none had), found the courage properly to tax the peasants (which is not done even now), and succeeded in making capitalists bring home the money they had exported abroad and change against Austrian kronen the foreign notes which they had hidden away (no one has yet discovered how this can be done by governmental decrees). But then a general election is going to be held in Austria this autumn [1923]; and on its eve one can hardly expect a political leader to give an impartial account of the work done by his chief and most successful opponent.

PRESIDENT MASARYK [1]

(*"The Times Literary Supplement," November 12th, 1925*)

MORALLY and mentally President Masaryk is one of the outstanding figures in the public life of Europe, while in Czechoslovakia his authority is supreme; he is now the uncontested leader of the nation and the keeper of its conscience.

President Masaryk was born poor, and as a boy was apprenticed to a locksmith; his education was for him an event and a struggle. Having taken his university degree, he thought of a diplomatic or political career, but had to rest content with the post of a university professor. His subject was philosophy, which attracted him in its more practical aspects; ethics, sociology and, most of all, the deeper problems of Czech national existence—in short, "unpolitical politics"—engaged his attention. His two chief assistants during the war, Dr. Beneš and Dr. Stefanik, were similarly ex-professors; but for each of these three Czechs the academic position itself had been a practical achievement. "I was

---

[1] "Die Welt-Revolution." Erinnerungen und Betrachtungen. By T. G. Masaryk. (Berlin: Erich Reiss Verlag.)

born poor," writes President Masaryk, " and never grew rich; thus I acquired a knowledge of men and life, and, in spite of theoretical work, became practical." At the age of about forty, in 1891, Masaryk entered the Austrian Parliament, but remained in it only two years. He felt oppressed by the sectarianism of the many small parties among the Czechs; moreover—" I was not ripe yet." Then followed fifteen years of study and travel; in 1907 he returned to Parliament, a lonely champion of unpopular or dimly apprehended causes, a party in himself. He was too fundamental and seemed too abstract to impress or lead the masses; only when the deepest problems of Czech national existence emerged in the war, by a complex process of selection, well known to history but not easy to trace, he became the national leader; not by " coming to the front," but by the Czech nation gathering to him. It was not his going abroad at the end of 1914 which made him the leader of the Czech revolutionary movement, but the uncompromising courage of his convictions had made him go abroad to lead it.

The position of the Czech nation was such that deep faith and a Puritanic contempt of material, seemingly insuperable, obstacles, a " categorical imperative " and the courage to follow it, were required for entering the path of " no compromise " by which the Czechs have once more attained Statehood. Even among educated people in Western Europe and America, very few knew anything about them. Masaryk soon realised how little the Czechs were known and how little account was taken of their existence; " I feared that nothing would be done for us in case of a speedy Allied victory." The immediate adversaries of the Czechs, Austria and the Magyars, were by no means unpopular in Western Europe. " There was no direct political hostility to Vienna as there was to Berlin. . . . Austria was generally looked upon as a counterweight to Germany and as a necessary organisation for its small nationalities and fractions of nations, a safeguard against Balkanisation." The chief craftsman of the Czech renaissance, the historian Palacky, himself had said about Austria that, if it did not exist, it would have to be invented; that phrase was now constantly thrown at Masaryk with a fine disregard of context, circumstances and later developments. Naturally Palacky had not wanted to see Austria broken up by the German Nationalists, and the Czechs engulfed in a Great Germany; but when he found that his idea of an Austria on a Slav basis had been an idle dream, Palacky himself turned to Russia, and with him the Czech nation. From the one Great Power which was Slav they now expected their liberation, and did not dare to criticise their big brother, not even in their thoughts. Liberals or Radicals at home, from a distance they worshipped at the shrine of Tsardom.

This was not the attitude of Masaryk, who knew and loved Russia with " conscious love." He loved the nation, but he knew that its system of government was pernicious and utterly inefficient. Masaryk, having left Austria in December 1914, did not turn to Russia, but to Western Europe; and he staked the future of the nation on the Western democracies, and not on Tsardom, as most of his countrymen would have done. Still, with him this was not a shrewd, accurate calculation, but mental honesty. The struggle against Austria was to him infinitely more than a mere political conflict; it was a moral issue, the battle of Huss and the Hussites, and of the Bohemian Brothers and Comenius, fought over once more. Again and again this point is emphasised in his Memoirs; it was a struggle against the Cæsaro-Papism of the Habsburgs, against the Jesuits and the political generals, against that combination of theocracy and bureaucracy, of Roman Catholic clericalism and mental and moral unfreedom, which were the very foundation of the Habsburg *régime*. But in fighting one semi-despotic theocracy, he could not turn for help to another, to Tsardom.

Such things would not stagger professional politicians; but Masaryk is a Puritan statesman.

His wanderings and labours during the war are recorded in the book, of which the spirit recalls to mind certain early New England diaries of men who, with ardent faith and small means, built the Church of the Lord in the wilderness. The story of Masaryk's work during the war is like his personality, simple, serious and sincere. He lived modestly, earned his living, did even the most tedious spade-work when required, carefully studied every aspect of the rapidly changing, complex world of politics, always kept the big issues in view and patiently worked for the cause of his people. In the meantime he tried to raise and maintain a pure spirit among those under his immediate leadership and to cleanse their community of internal discords; he did not allow them to accept subsidies from the Allied Powers; he taught them to rely on their own forces and to do the necessary work with whatever means they possessed. Finally—the greatest and most difficult of his labours—he set to work to raise a Czech national army in order to gain for the Czechs a place and weight among the nations. But the only recruiting-ground at his disposal, where considerable numbers of Czechs and Slovaks fit for military service could be found, was in the prisoner camps in Russia (and later on also in Italy). The men were ready to answer his call; but the legitimist spirit was so deeply engrained in Tsarist Russia that its officials and generals could not bring themselves to sympathise with a revolutionary movement, with war prisoners volunteering to fight against their own God-given Monarch. Promises were made to the Czechs, a statute was decreed for their army, and in the end nothing was done. It was only in the chaos of the Russian Revolution that the Czech volunteers could be gathered into one corps; but by that time little fighting was left to be done on the Russian front, and even the transport to France by Archangel had become too difficult and too risky. The Czech Legions now set out on their bold anabasis, to reach the French front by way of Siberia and America. But Masaryk could not stay with his men to the end; he had to hurry ahead to America with a view to making the necessary preparations for their further transport and in order to continue his political work, which he obviously could not carry on from the depths of Bolshevik Russia. He arrived at Washington in April 1918. When, in November 1918, he set out for England again, it was as President-elect of the new Czechoslovak Republic; and no one was more astonished at the change in his position than Masaryk himself. On December 21st he arrived at Prague to take up the heavy task of national reconstruction; "after having gone to see my wife in a nursing-home, I slept for the first time in the Prague Castle—*i.e.*, I did not sleep."

The sub-title of the book is "Reminiscences and Reflections," and it is the "reflections" which make it unique among war memoirs. Sociology, especially in its ethical aspects, had been the study of Masaryk's life; and the war was to him but an acute stage in the "chronic crisis" of modern civilisation, whose development he had watched during the preceding forty years. Throughout the book, in between the records of political events and activities, sketches are interspersed on the mental development and life of the various nations among which Masaryk had to work. There are a few masterly pages on mediæval and modern Italy; a chapter on France and its intellectual movements; a fine and remarkably impartial analysis of Russian Bolshevism, about which nothing seems to strike Masaryk more than its primitive crudeness. The chapters about England and America are less discerning and instructive, although Masaryk has a much older personal knowledge of the Anglo-Saxon countries than of France, which he had never visited before the war—so close is the affinity of the various national types on the European Continent and such is their distance from the Anglo-Saxons. Most important and deepest are the chapters on modern Germany, its " metaphysic Titanism " and " philosophic absolutism "; perhaps for the first time the path is here sketched which necessarily led from Goethe and Kant to Prussian militarism.

Had President Masaryk found the means clearly and conclusively to seize and to express the things present before his mind, this war book would have become one of the greatest works of our time. But when he approaches the summits of his thought, a region of cloud seems to intervene between him and the reader; the attempt to convey his own mental pictures and experiences breaks down, and he becomes in the deeper sense inarticulate. Then he seems to abandon the attempt fully to express his thought, and merely throws out a list of terms, names and references, as if he meant to say: " Take up these things, go through them carefully, compare and collate them, and you will see my meaning. I cannot explain any further." But there are very few indeed who can understand those references scattered throughout the immense realms of the world's literature, philosophy and political thought, or who can ever hope to follow them up. Various passages in this book will give invaluable incentive to thinkers and researchers; but, interesting as they are for the average reader, they fail to give him a clear, synthetic picture. He will close the book conscious of having been in touch with one of the master minds of our time, which has not, however, succeeded in fully expressing itself to the ordinary man.

THE VICTORY OF AN IDEA [1]

("The Observer," December 30th, 1928)

WHEN in 1914 Professor Masaryk, a lonely thinker, and Dr. Beneš, a young intellectual, took up the revolutionary struggle for the national independence of Czechoslovakia, they had nothing to build on except an idea. Prior to the war, the Czechoslovaks themselves had never clearly envisaged that programme which an historic catastrophe alone could bring within the range of possibility; and even then the political independence of a nation whose territory intervened between Berlin, Vienna and Budapest was bound to be the last thing which the Germanic Powers would concede. But anyhow in 1914 the Western Allies knew very little about the Czechs, and gave no thought to their future, while the Panslavism of Tsarist Russia was of an Orthodox and Balkanic, rather than of a Central European, character. The dismemberment of Austria-Hungary was not among the original war-aims of the Entente.

[1] "My War Memoirs." By Eduard Beneš. (George Allen and Unwin. 21*s*. net.)

THE VICTORY OF AN IDEA

By the patient labours of a century, the Czechs had risen from the poverty, illiteracy and oblivion which had been their condition since the defeat on the White Mountain in 1618, and by 1914 had attained a very satisfactory level of cultural development and material well-being, and even a certain influence in Austria's internal politics and administration. Were they now to stake their achievements and future on one single card, the value of which no one could possibly discern? Those alone dared to face the risk who, like Masaryk, admitted neither doubts nor compromise in matters of principle, and who, whilst carefully considering every step along their narrow path, refused to leave the choice of the path to prudential calculations. In November 1914, Dr. Beneš was told by one of the Czech party leaders that they

> "were mad, that Masaryk was leading the nation to another 'White Mountain' . . . that a politician who was responsible for a large party and, in fact, for the whole nation, could not and must not engage in such a gambling policy as that of Professor Masaryk. Besides, the plans which we had formed were fantastic. . . . He repeatedly asked where were the slightest guarantees from the Entente which would justify us in such a policy."

There were none; but to Professor Masaryk and Dr. Beneš the struggle against Vienna and Budapest was " first and foremost . . . a fundamental moral question."

> " As far as the Allies were concerned, our only guarantee could be the success of our revolutionary activities. . . . We simply had to thrust our cause into the main streams of world events, in the midst of which it would become too important a factor to be afterwards ignored."

Among the Czechs the work of the revolutionaries commanded the sympathy of all who came into touch with it and the unquestioning devotion of many. A Czech servant of the Austrian Minister of the Interior copied for them by night papers which he found with his master; Czech officials of the police informed them of what was happening in their offices; distinguished statesmen co-operated with them, and even the leader, who had condemned their policy as mad, twice warned Dr. Beneš when the police were after him. Hundreds of men, many in the Austrian Government service, knew something about their activities, but no one ever betrayed them. Masaryk stood for an idea which carried a moral appeal to every Czech; and it was that unpremeditated conspiracy of an entire nation which enabled him and Beneš to speak and act for it when they became *émigrés* in Allied countries. Hopeless as their cause appeared, in three years they succeeded in establishing their international position (of the new States, Czechoslovakia alone was invited to sign the Armistice as an Allied Power). They were honest and open in their dealings and yet shrewd, disinterested but full of resource; they did not force the pace, nor try to bargain while not in a position to do so. Everything they could procure—secret intelligence, a propaganda organisation, volunteers—they placed unreservedly and unconditionally at the service of the Allies; they skilfully avoided political entanglements in the maze of conflicting Allied interests; and they never lost courage, though their choice was mostly of difficulties.

The worst danger to their cause was that of a separate peace with the Habsburgs, either on the part of the Allies or of the Czechs in Austria. The Western Powers repeatedly dallied with that hopeless idea; and even more natural would this have been in Czech politicians at home, who saw the Central Powers victorious at the front, had no guarantees whatsoever from the Allies, and were plied with threats and offers from the Austrian Government. But such action would have ruined the position and the gains, as yet unconsolidated, of the Czech revolutionaries abroad. " You must not disavow us, or our cause is lost"—was their message continually repeated to Prague through secret channels; that they were not disavowed, proves once more the power of the idea for which they stood.

Meantime the one and only way in which they could firmly establish themselves among the Allies was by a volunteer army. In this they were successful, though the difficulties they had to contend with were enormous; even after having persuaded the Allied Governments to allow recruiting among Czech prisoners of war, they

> "nevertheless for a very long time, and in many cases up to the end of the war, encountered complete lack of understanding on the part of subordinate officials and local authorities. . . . Our prisoners must have been endowed with superhuman patience to achieve what they did, without giving up hope or surrendering to complete despair."

The goal was reached when, on August 9th, 1918, Great Britain acknowledged the Czechoslovaks as an Allied nation, their armies as Allied armies, and their National Committee, under the presidency of Professor Masaryk, as "the present trustee of the future Czechoslovak Government." From this process, says Dr. Beneš,

> "can be demonstrated how our State was established deliberately and step by step, by

laborious creative work, which had been planned with due regard to the political and psychological factors involved. This process of our gradual recognition by the Allies and our establishment by successive stages during the war provides much material which can be studied with advantage by all those who are concerned with the theories of sociology, law, and statesmanship."

Indeed, the lesson to be learned from it is what single individuals can achieve, when they act as keepers of the nation's conscience, and champion its cause in a single-minded, disinterested, and fearless manner.

ZIONISM

(" *The New Statesman*," November 5th, 1927)

EIGHTEEN hundred years we Jews have waited for the Messianic miracle and the return to our own land. It was that hope which imparted a peculiar meaning to our communal life and survival. We passed the endless centuries of vigil, fundamentally indifferent to the world around us, indifferent even to our own sufferings, in a state of suspended animation, with survival for our only aim. We believed that, on the day of the return, even the dead whom we buried in the Exile would rise from their graves and wander their last way to Palestine. We tried to found no permanent existence anywhere, we did not even plan our return, but waited for a miracle, conceived as miracles were in previous ages. This faith is now dying fast, and Israel has to face the practical problem of its existence and of its uncertain future—a stupendous process of reorientation in the oldest and most tenacious of races. Some of us find the solution in dissolution; others are determined actively to work for the " miracle " for which we have hitherto waited.

ZIONISM

Orthodox Jewry is a melting glacier and Zionism is the river which springs from it; evaporation and the river result from the same process, and are both its necessary results.

In Jewish orthodoxy, religion and nationality were identical; the loss of the Messianic hope logically leads to separation between them. Tradition still gives a national colouring to our religion and a religious colouring to our nationalism; but a Jewish religion has become possible which is merely a creed, and a Jewish nationalism which is purely political; whilst hundreds of thousands, and by no means the worst among us, taking no interest in theology and ritual and having lost touch with our national tradition, leave the Jewish community altogether and merge in the surrounding nations. Provided they do so without the self-abasement and the insult inherent in a denial of their origin, we have no reason to blame them; if community with us has no meaning for them, why should they remain with us? The lot of the Jew is such that without a powerful idea it cannot be borne with honour. In a "*testudo*" there is no room for anyone who will not hold up a shield.

In fact, dissolution and ultimate disappearance seem the inevitable future of the Jewries of Western and Central Europe; however much pleasure or anxiety the so-called Jewish question may provide even in these parts to obsessed anti-Semites, and however much wonder or discomfort their obsession may cause to us, there is here no real Jewish question, and without further immigration from Eastern Europe there would be, and there soon will be, no Jews. The orthodox Jews of Eastern Europe multiply quickly, not because their birth-rate is higher than that of their neighbours—it is invariably lower—but because of a lower infantile mortality. But once the religious bar to birth control has disappeared, the same care for the children produces with the Jews a limitation of families far stricter even than it is with the French; and whilst there is no excess of births over deaths among educated Jews, baptisms and inter-marriages dissolve the stock—in Hamburg and Berlin there is about one mixed marriage to every two Jewish marriages. We have no religious statistics in this country, but anyone can gain a picture of this process of dissolution by considering the Jews (and half-Jews) of his own acquaintance. Still, the Jews of Western and Central Europe form only about two millions out of fifteen—these are the fringes of the glacier from which no river can spring and by which one must not judge the nature and future of the glacier itself.

The two numerically important bodies in Jewry are the seven million, mostly Yiddish-speaking, Jews of Eastern Europe (almost three millions in Poland, over two and a half in Russia, one in Roumania, the rest in Lithuania, Latvia and Carpatho-Russia), and the three and a half million Jews in the United States, the majority of them immigrants from Eastern Europe or children of such immigrants—about 2,400,000 Jews entered the U.S.A. between 1881 and 1924. This sudden mass immigration is now abruptly cut off, and it is difficult as yet to form a judgment about the future of the Jews in America. So much, however, is certain, that those settled over there will remain in the country, that they are rising in wealth and education, and that the phenomena known among the Jews of Western and Central Europe—a low birth-rate, intermarriages and baptisms—have already set in, and will in time make appreciable inroads on the stock. Another effect of this migration deserves attention. Before the war the million Jews inhabiting Germany and Western Austria formed the most important body of educated, wealthy Jews in the world, and consequently with them lay the intellectual and financial leadership in Jewry. This is now passing to the American Jews, while the Palestine Mandate has fixed in London the political leadership of Jewish nationalism. In other words, the centre of gravity in Jewry has moved from the German to the English-speaking countries. The main body of Jews, whose existence forms the real Jewish question, remains in Eastern Europe; the Jews primarily called upon to deal with the problem live in America and in England.

In Eastern Europe the nature of the problem is not the same in different countries. In Russia it is now primarily economic; Bolshevism, while destroying the livelihood of the Jewish masses in the so-called "Pale"—small traders and artisans —has disorganised Russia's economic system, which could otherwise easily absorb her Jews in a productive manner. Still, supremely bad as the position is at present, there is room for these people and there are possibilities—witness the effective work of colonisation which American Jews are now conducting and financing in Southern Russia. In Roumania the problem is primarily political; her Jews could live and prosper were they allowed to. In Poland, it is both political and economic, which renders the position of her Jews desperate. The country is over-populated; the Jews form a distinct type and a separate community; their numbers are such that, even were there the wish (which there is now on neither side), they could not possibly be assimilated to the Poles in the way common among the nations of Western and Central Europe. Before the war, Poles and Jews alike emigrated in hundreds of thousands; the outlets are now stopped; the possibilities of livelihood are narrowed down; the Poles, to put it mildly, do not like the Jews. It does not worry them if the Jews go to the wall, and as economic life is coming more and more under control, they have hundreds of means in their country to drive the Jews that way. Some find pleasure in it, others do so because they require the place of the Jews for themselves. Where will this end if no outlet is found in time for a new Jewish emigration?

With the loss of the Messianic hope the passivity of orthodox Jewry breaks down. We have to find our own place on earth and live as other people do. Where the Jews live in dense masses, speak their own language, and form a distinct community, they have their own " nationality," whether they profess it or not; anyhow, they are treated as strangers by their neighbours. It is not true that it is the rise of a conscious Jewish nationality which raises a bar between them; the bar exists anyhow, and a national consciousness merely gives the Jews a backbone and relieves them of the feeling of moral inferiority, which some of their neighbours like to inflict on them however much they may loathe its natural consequences—aggressive cringing and pushing. Zionism, whatever possibilities it may open up in future, cannot alone within measurable time solve the economic problems of East-European Jewry which cry out for solution; but it can even now help to create an atmosphere in which other remedies will become more effective. A consciousness of nationality, of national purpose and responsibility, of the duty to work for a common future and the duty to become normal after eighteen centuries of abnormal life, are in themselves of imponderable value, for along the whole line, in matters economic, national or communal, an end must be made to that nondescript character which the endless detached waiting has produced in great masses of our people.

Possibly a majority of national Jews will have to remain for ever in the Diaspora, but, even so, there must be somewhere a National Home to give them normality—every nation must somewhere have its own territorial centre. There are many more Irishmen scattered throughout the world than inhabiting the Irish Free State, and yet its existence, though they may never see it, is of supreme importance to them; it gives them a standing among other nations. Our very survival was inherently bound up with the hope of a return to Palestine. The passive hope has now changed into an active will; those of us who still adhere to the idea which for eighteen hundred years stood in the centre of our thinking, have to work for that which we no longer expect to come to us in another way. No one who looks with an unprejudiced eye at the road which the Jewish people has covered, at the sufferings which it has patiently borne, at the spiritual strength it has shown, and lastly at the desperate position in which a large part of it is now placed, can doubt the driving force which there is behind the Zionist movement.

It is now [in 1927] ten years since the Balfour Declaration opened the gate which hitherto had been practically closed to us; the Mandate has given a definite international status to our work. We have started upon it. Since 1922 the Jewish population of Palestine has doubled, and now amounts to almost 160,000; we have founded a number of agricultural settlements and have started new industries; tens of thousands of Jews, who in Eastern Europe would now be beggars without profession, have learnt to work. But so far we have not been altogether successful. In 1925, when America finally closed up against immigration and the economic crisis became acute in Poland, there was an inrush with which we proved unable to cope; we have suffered a setback, and had to take stock of means and methods. The way to increase the possibilities for immigration will be found; under modern conditions the possibilities of each country are what men make them—did Middlesex or Manhattan Island inherently and unmistakably show the possibilities for settlement which we now see in them? If Palestine is to be our National Home—and we now can see no other on the globe nor in all our history—we must not even ask what will be the price at which we can achieve it.

Other nations, when their existence or perhaps only their interests were threatened, spent thousands of millions of pounds on war. The wealth of the Jewish community, with half the East-European Jewry downright paupers, is *per capita* less than that of England, France or America, and we bear at least a proportionate share in the burdens of other nations. Still, at this time, when a crisis of unequalled seriousness has supervened after the eighteen centuries of suspended animation, we must not inquire into the magnitude of the sacrifice which we may be called upon to make. Lord Balfour, when defending in the House of Lords the Palestinian policy of the Government, expressed the hope that their Lordships would never sink to " that unimaginative depth " which excludes experiment or adventure. We Jews certainly must not do so; for should the enterprise in which the British Empire and the Jewish nation are partners fail, to our friends in Great Britain, perhaps the best we have had since Cyrus and Alexander (we can use quaint comparison, as our memory is long), this would be a disappointment, for ourselves a catastrophe of truly immeasurable consequence. And perhaps even the outside world would then find that a spiritual catastrophe in Jewry cannot remain a matter of indifference to other nations.

THEODOR HERZL

(" *The Monthly Pioneer*," *February* 1929)

RELIGIOUS Zionism is as old as the Exile, and enduring as the sufferings of the Jews, and it lives in the faith itself; but modern political Zionism has its founder in Theodor Herzl, the man who first attempted to express the oldest national idea in the language of our own age. He formulated some of its fundamental conceptions and aims, but hardly realised what labour the task would require, and the way in which it would have to be achieved. With deep respect the Zionist takes up the Memoirs of Herzl; and yet little more than an antiquarian interest would by now attach to them, were it not that they mark the distance which the movement has traversed since his time.

Herzl's Memoirs [1] cover the nine years from 1895, when the idea of the Jewish National State first entered his life, till his death in 1904. They are of an unvarnished frankness, and record his strivings and failures, his thoughts, feelings and

[1] "Theodor Herzl's Tagebücher." 3 vols. (Jüdischer Verlag, Berlin.)

even his day-dreams, such as imaginative people experience but seldom put down on paper. His personality is reflected in the book. Here is a *littérateur*, an enthusiast, sincere and persevering, skilful and unpractical, clever and naive, sometimes inspired and at other times ridiculous, who in the end has made history. There was real force behind his often fanciful schemes, " sufficient to propel heavy machines and send men wandering "—" *die Judennot* " (the misery of being a Jew). Jew-baiting, once more a pastime of the masses and a useful weapon for politicians, had re-awakened the Jew in Herzl and set him dreaming of a Jewish State " where bent noses, black or red beards, and bow-legs will not render us despicable forthwith ; where at last we shall live free on our own land and die peacefully in our own homes ; where we too shall be honoured for great deeds."

The Jewish State is an idea born of sufferings which call up half-forgotten and long-neglected traditions, and rests on imponderables which weigh most in the destinies of nations. " Great things require no fixed foundations. An apple needs support, but the earth floats in the universe. Perhaps I shall found and fix the Jewish State without any firm support." " To-day I am a lonely individual," wrote Herzl in 1895, " to-morrow possibly the spiritual leader of hundreds of thousands. Anyhow the author and apostle of a powerful idea." And again, two years later, after the first Zionist Congress: " Now, at Basle, I have founded the Jewish State. If to-day I said this aloud I should be laughed at, but perhaps in five, certainly in fifty years everybody will see it. It is the will of the nation which makes the State . . . and, even where it has its territory, the State is always something abstract."

Ardent and prophetic, Herzl was, none the less, frequently superficial in his conceptions and ideas. He imagined that a nation could be made by diplomacy, transported to any suitable vacant territory, and established on an ingenious, well-planned scheme. He did not see the deeper, sacred meaning of the reunion of the Jews to their great Mother, the Promised Land. To him the " New Land " of his dreams did not necessarily mean Palestine, and he never came fully to understand that Palestine alone could become the focusing-point of Jewish nationalism—for every " house of bondage " has its flesh-pots as well as its sufferings, and it requires something more than the mere desire to have finished with its humiliations to make the Jews incur the inevitable hardships and privations of a new and unwonted life. Herzl, born at Budapest and educated in Vienna, had grown up in the discoloured and discolouring surroundings of Central European town life, where comparatively small communities of educated Jews, no longer rooted in the faith and no more in touch with the Jewish masses, tended to succumb to the nondescript, standardised average which is typical of modern Germany and her intellectual satellites. The idea of a return to Palestine had to come to him from outside, from English Puritans, our co-heirs to the Old Testament, and from the Yiddish-speaking Jews of Eastern Europe, whose knowledge of geography does not extend to the Argentine, Uganda and Timbuctoo, but knows one distinction only—between the sacred Erets Israel (Land of Israel) and the infinite, inhospitable Galuth (the Exile).

There is a legend in the Talmud that the burning bush from which the voice of the Lord spoke to Moses was the Nation of Israel gathered at the foot of Mount Sinai. But Herzl never fully understood the live power which there is in the masses, though occasionally he would speak of calling them up to self-help, "as no one wants to help them." He had grown up in the old Austria, where everything was obtained by backstairs methods from the "governing circles," and, having had no intimate experience of politics, did not know how very little the mighty can do, how little they dare, how they play with ideas but seldom act on them, except when forced by circumstances or the will of the masses.

Herzl started by going the round of the Jewish multi-millionaires, Baron Hirsch, the Rothschilds, and the *Alliance Israélite*, rightly explaining to them that munificent charity, unless guided by a great idea, tends to pauperise its recipients; but even if they listened with attention to his critical remarks, being practical, and possibly unimaginative, men, when informed of Herzl's excessively ingenious, elaborate schemes, they did not wish to continue or resume the discussion. Next he went the round of princes and Ministers; talked to the Grand Duke of Baden, a fine, religious man, with a deep appreciation of sincere idealism; to the German Emperor, who waxed enthusiastic at the prospect of theatricals during his impending visit to Palestine, but drew back at the first obstacle; to the cynical German Chancellor, Prince Bülow, who knew that the Berlin Jews of his acquaintance " would not leave the Stock Exchange," while the others " had no money "; to the Russian Ministers, Plehve and Witte, who recognised that Jewish nationalism would draw the Jewish masses away from revolutionary movements, but found themselves unable to further Herzl's schemes; to the Sultan and the political demi-monde in and round Constantinople, all alike intent on bribes varying merely in size, and keen to get money without delivering the goods; to the King of Italy, who was friendly and very reasonable; and even to the Pope. Once only on his pilgrimage round the capitals of Europe did Herzl reach a practical point and meet with an earnest wish to do something for the Jews—in the negotiations with Mr. Joseph Chamberlain and Lord Lansdowne; but the scheme of colonising the Sinai Peninsula foundered over the irrigation problem.

Meantime, the Jewish masses, especially in Eastern Europe, gathered to the Zionist banner; the movement was rapidly gaining in weight, broadening in outlook, becoming more intense, and at the same time more practical in its conceptions; in the Diaspora itself it produced a Jewish Renaissance. Then came the War, the Balfour Declaration, new persecutions in Eastern Europe, the closing up of America to immigration, and at last a chance for work in Palestine. And by now little, if anything, is left in Zionism of the naive schemes and showy displays of Herzl's day-dreams, though the fundamental idea of re-integration in a National Home remains. Would he be proud or disappointed could he now see the movement of which he was the first exponent? Probably both; anyhow, he would have to learn and unlearn a good deal before he could appreciate the work and ideas of his own followers. There is a Jewish legend that Moses on Mount Sinai, when seeing the Lord adorn the letters of the Hebrew alphabet with crowns and points, asked Him why He did it? "Some day," answered the Lord, "a man will come, Akiba ben Joseph, and from these crowns and points he will draw various doctrinal deductions." Moses asked to be shown the man; but when he heard Akiba instructing disciples, he saddened, for he understood nothing. Then a disciple asked Akiba: "Wherefrom do you derive this knowledge, Rabbi?" And Akiba replied: "This is a tradition handed down to us from Moses on Mount Sinai."

AGRARIAN REVOLUTION

(" *The Manchester Guardian Commercial*," "*Reconstruction in Europe.*" *August* 1922)

THE man "who grows the turnips" seemed immensely important to Ruskin, who was fortunate enough not to see him come into his own.

Before the war the "rural exodus" was a subject of general (and futile) regret in Europe and America alike. Practically everywhere the wages of rural labour were lower than those paid in towns, not in money terms alone, but even when measured in purchasing power. Improvements in means and methods were reducing the amount of labour required to bring forth the necessary raw materials, and an increasing proportion was set free to engage in the "refining" processes or in the production of those further values which, for good or for bad, form the essence of civilisation. It is a condition, and in turn a result, of material progress that fewer men should be seen engaged in "growing turnips." But when the authority and the organisation on which modern society rests break down, when mutual confidence weakens and the system of exchange gets deranged, when trains cease to run according to time-tables, food and raw materials grow scarce, and factories can no longer keep up their normal production, then theoretical speculations and thought are at a discount, an increasing number of material objects come to rank as luxuries of doubtful utility, and the man who grows the turnips and can feed himself (and others if he chooses) is master. There is a stage in the retrograde development known as general paralysis, when only by a supreme effort the human being still manages to walk on two legs, and there is a stage in social paralysis when all the efforts of the community have to be concentrated once more on securing for it its indispensable food-supply. No one needs then to fear any further exodus from the self-satisfied, self-sufficient villages to the " useless " towns. This is the condition which, in varying degrees, the war produced in Central and Eastern Europe.

Wars, by destroying organisation and accumulated wealth and by reducing society to a more primitive condition, raise the importance of the agrarian classes, which, moreover, profit by the devaluation of the currencies, being as a rule burdened with mortgages and debts rather than with bank balances. At the same time wars, by loosening the ties of society, open the road for revolutions. In their results they are both retrograde and revolutionary, which implies no contradiction. For revolutions are in their very nature economically and socially retrograde: and this is the reason why, so far, agrarian revolutions alone have been successful. The French Revolution of 1789 was essentially agrarian, and its land settlement was its most permanent achievement. The Revolution of 1848 failed in France because it had no agrarian programme, and in Germany and Austria it succeeded only in so far as it was agrarian. The forces behind the Russian Revolution of 1917 were agrarian, and there the victorious agrarian revolution now gradually destroys other conquests incompatible with its own principles and nature. The German Revolution of 1918 was essentially urban, and that is why its victory is uncertain and its social achievements are nil.

The masses are invincible whenever they have a clearly defined, feasible aim in view. The Socialist programme of the industrial labour movement cannot be realised immediately, but agrarian programmes are usually capable of immediate realisation. This accounts for the enormous strength of revolutionary peasantries. Socialist production would require a higher degree of organisation than now exists, or even than we seem able to devise and work at the present time. Revolutions which come because the social organisation has been weakened, and which, in turn, weaken it still further, clearly cannot produce that higher, as yet unknown, organisation. Agrarian revolutions, on the other hand, either leave the existing system of production virtually untouched, merely effecting changes in distribution—when they free the peasant farmer from feudal dues or transfer the property in land from a rent-collecting landlord to the man who actually tills it; or they mark a descent to lower, well-known forms of production—when they break up big agrarian enterprises, highly organised on a capitalist basis, and hand over the land to peasants who will work it in ways known since times immemorial. This is what is actually happening over a vast expanse of Eastern and Central Europe.

Industrial labour, if by injudicious action it impairs its own productiveness, runs the danger of losing its markets, employment and livelihood. But the peasant, by seizing the land of the big estates, may increase his own share in foodstuffs while diminishing the total agricultural production of the country. He will be the last to suffer hunger. He starts by cutting the branches on which other people sit, and he is most revolutionary when he is least productive. Where individual care counts for more than acreage, smallholdings and even allotments may prove superior to big estates—in market-gardening, fruit growing, poultry-farming and to some extent even dairying and the raising of cattle. But this kind of agriculture depends on big towns or densely populated industrial districts for its markets, and under their influence the more productive type of farm wins the day; and little is heard of revolutionary movements among the agrarian population in the neighbourhood of big cities. But where the big farm offers the more favourable conditions—*e.g.* in the production of cereals, sugar-beet or potatoes—it is, nevertheless, unable, at least in Eastern Europe, to oust the peasant. On the contrary, even there the land-hungry peasant who does not calculate what interest his land yields to him, who, indeed, does not even calculate the value of his own labour when applied to his own land, has in the past succeeded in buying up the land of the big landowners in the open market (frequently with money earned in Germany, the United States, or Canada). But this was a laborious, slow process. Now that the war, by weakening social authority and organisation, has opened the road to revolution, the peasant sees a possibility of completing the process of breaking up the big landed estates and of acquiring his own patch of land in a much easier manner—by political methods, through legislation which he dictates to subservient Governments in Parliaments dominated by his own representatives.

In Western Europe the peasants are much-admired champions of conservatism; Eastern Europe continues to produce Jack Straws and their jacqueries. A most important frontier, not recorded on any map, separates these two parts of Europe. It is the line of demarcation between the region of scattered farms in the west and of clustered villages in the east. Where the scattered farms stand in the midst of their own fields each farm is an economic unit which hardly ever will be subdivided on the death of its owner. Where the peasant population lives in clustered villages the peasant holding usually consists of a number of strips of land scattered in the open fields, which thus do not form a unit and offer no natural barrier to subdivision; anyhow, no truly rational system of agriculture can be pursued on these scattered strips. When serfdom was abolished sufficient land was assigned to the peasants in most countries of Eastern Europe. But each subsequent generation has added new huts to the clustered village, and by subdivision reduced the size of the average peasant holding. The owners of self-sufficient peasant farms supply the type of conservative peasant. Those of dwarf holdings cry out for more land, which

AGRARIAN REVOLUTION

can be obtained in no other way than by breaking up the surviving demesnes; they supply the revolutionary element dominant among the East European peasantries.

Before the war the manor-houses on the big landed estates were centres of high culture and mainstays of modern economic life in Eastern Europe. They resembled Roman villas in semi-barbaric lands. Their inhabitants read the works and thought the thoughts of the most advanced civilisation in the midst of an illiterate peasantry. The estates were worked, if not always in a scientific manner, anyhow with more science and much better machinery than any peasant could supply to his holding. They produced big quantities of cereals for sale and served as basis for various agricultural industries, such as, *e.g.*, the beet-sugar industry. From these estates the towns derived a considerable part of their food supply, and trade practically all its exports. On the big estates the peasants earned money wages with which they bought manufactures. This trade will to a large extent disappear together with the latifundia, especially in districts far removed from big towns. Perhaps the peasantry in the villages, or at least certain portions of it, will be better fed and housed, but the level of economic culture, and still more of intellectual culture, will sink low. The " Cham " (the descent from Noah's third son is ascribed to the peasant in Eastern Europe) has conquered within the village at a time when the villages have vanquished the towns. The destruction of wealth and the devaluation of money in the French Revolutionary and Napoleonic wars, by weakening the towns, prepared the ground for the subsequent reaction, which was, however, culturally relieved, not aggravated, by the survival and dominance of the educated feudal classes. There will be little to relieve the darkness of the new peasant democracies of Eastern Europe. Nor will the disappearance of the squire usher in the millennium even into the village itself. He may be succeeded by big peasants owning considerable farms; but these big peasants are infinitely harder taskmasters for the village labourers than the average squire. Or the subdivision of land will continue; then the peasant will soon find himself reduced once more to a very precarious condition; moreover, without any longer being able to supplement his income with wages earned on the demesne.

Outside Russia economic difficulties are at present to some extent retarding the break-up of the big landed estates. Most peasants, even if given the land free, would hardly be able to set up their farms, for lack of capital. But sooner or later this break-up of latifundia must come, for in almost every State of Eastern or East-Central Europe the peasants have established their own political power or even dominion, and this they are determined to use for the realisation of their economic programme. They can make and unmake Governments. They impose their will on the Governments, whatever philosophical or social principles these Governments may profess. In Russia and in Poland alike the Government tried to regulate trade in foodstuffs with a view to protecting the town population—its own officials, the intelligentsia, and the industrial workmen— against the food-usury of the agrarian classes. The Soviet Government had finally to capitulate before the peasants and to admit free trade in foodstuffs; and a few weeks later the same concession had to be made to the peasants on the other side of the *cordon sanitaire*, in Poland. Elemental economic forces are at work which no theories of the educated classes can touch or efficiently control, and which are preparing a similar future for all East European countries.

The peasant has conquered. A radical in so far as the land question is concerned, he is otherwise mediæval in his thinking, egoistic and exclusive in his class feeling, brutal and narrow. Little respect he has now left for the squire, but certainly none at all for the town intelligentsia. The squirearchy represent a conservative, and the town intelligentsia a more radical, type of civilisation. The war has sapped the position of both, and since the war the two have competed for the political support of the peasants, as if the peasant in defeating the one meant to establish the other. In reality both types are sinking fast at the conquering touch of the peasant, and with them falls the cultural level of Eastern Europe.

Hierarchical, traditional Churches alone, especially the Roman Catholic Church, in countries such as Poland can share in the victory of the peasants. True, the clergy will lose their land. " It will help them in their prayers and pious meditations," says the peasant, " if they are relieved of worldly cares; and farming is very anxious business." But then the matters of the spirit the peasants are prepared to leave to them. A humiliated *ci-devant* aristocrat may be hired for the Foreign Office, a tame, middle-class intellectual for the Ministry of Finance, a priest or an agent of the clergy will look after education; the Home Office and the Ministry of Agriculture the peasant will retain in his own heavy fist. There was a time when the divine right of kings protected a growing lay culture against the encroachments of a militant Church and when feudal lords, a caste capable of developing culture, of appreciating it and of paying for it, levied a toll on the illiterate classes. In a Catholic peasant republic no divine authority is left in the State, but all divine authority is apt to centre in the hierarchical, traditional Church, itself run by priests of peasant extraction and low culture; and there is no room for a leisured class of independent means and of an independent spirit. The peasant democracy of the Canton of Lucerne in 1845 submitted its new constitution for approval to the Pope. Perfect theocracies may yet arise in Eastern Europe in the dark shadow of the " conquering Cham."

THE PEASANT AND THE STATE

("*The Spectator,*" *June 27th*, 1925)

WHEN Stambuliski, the Bulgarian peasant Premier (vanquished and killed by those who now govern the country), was returning home from the Genoa Conference, he was met at Tirnovo station by the prefect of the district. "Are there any rich people in the town?" asked Stambuliski. "Yes, there are some." "Are they all in prison?" was the next question. "No, sir . . ." replied the perplexed prefect. "Why aren't they?" Stambuliski was not a Bolshevik: far from it; he was a peasant. "*Qui non est agricola, num potest salvari?*"

The Russian peasant has answered the question in the (expected) negative. "Christians" (*krestyanye*) in Russian are the peasants alone; the priest himself is not a *krestyanin*. A new word had to be formed—*khrystyanin*—linguistically to reinclude the others in the Christian community. But to the peasant they are hardly God's children. This is one reason why Bolshevism could win, but cannot work.

All other classes are to the peasant mere parasites living on his labour, and he would gladly do without them (he did not wait for Karl Marx or Lenin to teach him the theory of "surplus-value"). He was before they had come into existence, and will be after they are buried in the earth which they do not work nor know, but which he possesses. "When Adam delved and Eve span, where was then the gentleman?" At Marlborough, in Wiltshire, the Inn of the Five Alls till recently bore witness to the ideas held when England was a predominantly agrarian country. "I rule over all," proclaimed the king on the sign; "I fight for all," said the knight; "I pray for all," professed the clergyman; "I plead for all," declared the lawyer; "I pay for all," answered them the peasant farmer.

By now we have forgotten in England what peasantries are like, we do not understand their immense, passive strength and their tragic, though natural, incapacity for government. In Ireland we incline to ascribe to the Irish character much which is common to all peasantries. We are faced by peasant communities in the East, but pay excessive attention to *babus* and *effendis* who could be silenced and ignored by anyone who knew how to handle the peasant masses. Questions of land tenure, not nationality or constitutional problems, move peasant communities.

"We have survived the cholera, we shall survive the Constitution," declared a Slav peasant member in the Austrian Parliament about 1867.

In 1789, Louis XVI called upon the nation to compile *cahiers* of its grievances. To bid people carefully to consider what ails them is the height of folly in any rulers; to call upon an over-burdened peasantry critically to examine its burdens is to ask for revolution. Napoleon knew better; he gave the peasant what he wanted, but did not ask him to think or vote. In the Concordat Napoleon and the Pope sacrificed friends and principles; the interests of the French peasant alone were treated as sacrosanct. He got the best of both worlds, his land on earth and his place in heaven, the estates of the Church which he had seized, and the services of the Church which had been withdrawn from him since he had seized its possessions. After that who could with him compete against Napoleon? On his return from Elba, Napoleon said to Benjamin Constant: "*Je ne suis pas, comme on l'a dit, l'empereur des soldats; je suis celui . . . des paysans de France . . .*"

More frequently, however, the support which the peasants give to a government is of a purely passive character: they just tolerate it. That is why the corrupt, "impious" Directory could survive so long in France and the Soviets now survive in Russia—both as an evil which is less than a return of the *émigré* big landowners. The State, like everything made by men, is constructed and run by those who need it and who are prepared to pay for it. The landed gentry in England, and still more the merchants, required a State organisation; hence the original combination of landowners and boroughs in the English Parliament. To modern industrial labour the State is a primary factor in their daily existence; it is therefore they who have forced open the way for democracy. The interest of the peasant in the State is too remote to make him an active, positive element in it; no big State has ever been built up by a peasantry, nor can be worked by them. Their hours of work are regulated by the sun and the weather, and the returns of their labour are determined by the soil and the seasons. The benefits they possibly derive from the State they hardly perceive, but they know it as tax-collector and recruiting-sergeant. The other classes are children of the State, stand in need of it every day of their lives, could not exist without the elaborate organisation which it provides and maintains; the peasant alone, the son of the earth, is anterior to the State; he could, if need be, revert to self-sufficiency, and can therefore afford to be an anarchist, without the effects of his action immediately and fatally recoiling on his own head. Nevertheless, he will bear burdens, so long as they appear to him part of fixed creation and he, in his organic conservatism, is not compelled or invited to consider their purpose. If they become excessive, if change destroys his faith in the inherent necessity of the existing order, if other classes teach the peasant the way to effect their own destruction, he rises in his immense, tenacious strength, and they have to bear the consequences. A wood once destroyed cannot grow up again in the Russian steppes unless carefully protected; the exuberant growth of grass and weeds keeps the sun and air from the young trees in spring, and the drought kills them in summer or the storms in winter. But grass can be destroyed and will always come up again with the returning season. The trees are the superstructure of society and the grass is the peasantry, closer to the earth, dense, invincible and indestructible in its numbers.

In the war, the peasant masses of Eastern and East-Central Europe were made to fight for causes which were strange and incomprehensible to them. The burden was excessive, their patience broke, and the peasant armies, one after another, suffered disruption—first the Russian, next the Bulgarian and Austro-Hungarian armies. With the armies broke down the State organisations. The peasant now asserts himself, and by agrarian revolution or so-called " reform " he gains exclusive possession of the land, which is all he cares for. He believes in private property and is conservative indeed—of anything he can lay hands on. Political power as such is of no interest to him except as a means for obtaining the land or avoiding taxation. This he can do now that " democracy " has made him dominant in all the agrarian countries of Europe. And this is their great problem: never before were State organisations shaken to the degree they have been now; never before were the financial burdens, which weigh them down, even approximately as heavy as they now are; never before was so great a part of national wealth concentrated in the hands of the peasants as is now in the agrarian communities of Europe; never before was the power of the peasants, a negative element in the State, what it is under modern democracy. Feudalism was once the force which made the peasant masses subservient to the interests of the community and made the countryside yield something besides turnips. What is now to replace it?

The miserable condition of finance in most Continental States is the direct result of the peasant's indifference towards the State and of the power which he has obtained over it; he practically sabotages the State and the other classes of society. Parliaments which depend on his vote do not dare to tax him properly—this is as true of France as of Poland or Yugo-Slavia. Indeed, there is an inherent difficulty in applying, *e.g.* the income tax, to the largely self-sufficient economy of the peasant proprietor. We hear a good deal about the absurdity of the high tariff walls put up by the agrarian Succession States. But it is no good preaching to them the obvious truth that their economic interest lies in developing agriculture and exchanging its rich produce against manufactured goods. They have to raise a revenue, and, not daring to tax the peasant openly, have to do so by roundabout methods which he does not understand or cannot directly resist. The imports which pass the frontiers contribute revenue; industries which grow up behind the tariff walls, however wasteful and wretched, add a taxable class to the population. The towns once more have to bear the main financial burdens, which have become fearfully heavy; and the dominant peasant has even less understanding for the needs of towns and civilisation than had kings and feudal lords. We witness a most extraordinary situation; small groups of educated men or town dwellers endeavour to reconstruct modern society and run modern States in the face of the passive obstruction of the dominant peasants who fundamentally have no use for either.

CURRENCIES AND EXCHANGES IN AN EAST GALICIAN VILLAGE

(" *The Manchester Guardian Commercial*," " *Reconstruction in Europe*," *April* 20*th*, 1922)

In the sixteenth century subjects were made to accept the religion of their rulers, now they have to take the paper money. But " Accept from Cæsar . . ." is a difficult and indeed bewildering precept when the impositions of the masters grow and their persons change.

Many armies have marched across East Galicia since August 1914, destroying wealth and building up Governments, requisitioning goods and passing off banknotes. Before 1914 East Galicia had for generations remained under Austrian rule. In September 1914 it was occupied by the Russians. In the summer of 1915 most of it was reconquered by the Austrian and German armies. In 1916 the Russians re-occupied part of the territory abandoned by them during the previous year. In 1917 the entire province passed once more under Austrian administration. In October 1918 came the collapse of the Habsburg Monarchy. Thereupon the East Galician

Ukrainians established their own Government. By July 1919 the Poles had completely conquered the country. In the summer of 1920 East Galicia came for a few weeks under Bolshevik occupation. Now [in 1922] it is again under the Poles. But in international law it is "No Man's Land," or rather the property of the Principal Allied and Associated Powers, to whom Austria has ceded it in the Treaty of St. Germain, a fact which is almost universally ignored or forgotten, as of all claimants to East Galicia the Western Powers alone (to the lively regret of the local population) have failed to supply the country with their own banknotes.

Until 1914 the East Galician peasant had known none but the Austrian money, and hardly realised the existence of other currencies. There were the silver guldens and crowns with the head of the old Emperor, and the banknotes depicting various allegorical females—but of these the identity did not trouble the mind of the East Galician peasant. Indifference to meaning is the perfect test of faith; and that unquestioning faith he naturally had in a currency which formed part of the settled scheme of his life, and, being stable, did not force him to think about monetary problems.

In 1914, with the Russian armies, before which the Austrians had fled in a panic, and with the new Government, more powerful than the highest authority which the East Galician peasant had hitherto known under the sun, came in the rouble. To that coin and banknote the peasant now gave the honour which was due unto the victorious Cæsar. Throughout the world foreign exchanges mathematically express an elaborate equation of hopes, doubts and fears, of political beliefs and calculations, of respect and disrespect for Governments. In East Galicia the rouble ranked high above the Austrian crown. Even the return of the Austrians failed to convince the East Galician peasant of their power or to make him believe in the permanency of their régime. He listened to the booming of the guns and watched the rapid rise in prices, and though he understood but little of politics and strategy, and still less about monetary inflation, he felt that his old standard of values could not be fully trusted any longer. He hoarded his precious roubles, and waited. He would take a rouble note, however dirty and torn, an Austrian crown only provided it was whole, smooth and clean.

By November 1918 both Cæsars had disappeared, and Governments which had sprung up over-night now claimed the power to create currencies and values. *Hrivni* and *karbovantsi* came in from the Russian Ukraine, the money of the democratic Peasant Republic. This the

Republican armies forced on the Polish big landowners and the Jewish traders, but so long as it was possible they paid their own peasants in Austrian crowns, which came to be honoured again. The hrivna was to have been equal to an Austrian crown, but even under the Ukrainian administration 100 hrivni were paid for 60 to 70 crowns. The naive claim appeared on the hrivni that they ranked " on an equality with gold," but the Austrian crowns were truly a reminiscence of a golden age, the symbol of a once-firmly-established order.

The Polish conquest of East Galicia, in the summer of 1919, opened up the country to the west, and closed it to the east. The Ukrainian hrivni lost all value. At first the Poles retained the Austrian crowns. But soon they began to introduce their own marks, to which, with fine foresight, the East Galician peasant gave the name of " Polish hrivni." They did not claim gold parity, but bore upon their face a quaintly worded guarantee: " The Polish State assumes the obligation to redeem this banknote in the future Polish currency at a rate of exchange to be fixed by the Legislative Assembly." There was nothing to indicate what its holder could expect to receive, but this undefined quantity was vouched for by the Polish nation. On most of the banknotes, opposite the inscription, appears

IN AN EAST GALICIAN VILLAGE

Kosciuszko, sad and despondent. " What is the good of his guarantee ? " asks the East Galician peasant. " He died long ago." So did the Queen Yadviga, who appears on some of the other banknotes, but then she has a crown on her head, which inspires some confidence in the East Galician peasant.

Early in 1920 the Poles, with a view to unifying their currency, fixed the rate of exchange between the inherited Austrian crown and the new Polish mark, and decided to withdraw the crown from circulation. The statutory rate of exchange of 100 crowns to 70 marks was from the very beginning unduly disadvantageous to the crown, and became even more so when the Polish Government, by vigorous printing, reduced the mark to a small fraction of its origin value. Consequently the East Galician peasant, who, thanks to the (frequently expensive) tuition received from the Jewish dealers, was rapidly developing into an expert on currencies, refused to part with his Austrian crowns at the statutory rate. More favourable location for these was found by illicit money-dealers beyond the borders of East Galicia and Poland. In accordance with the Treaty of St. Germain, the Succession States of Austria-Hungary proceeded (at various dates) to stamp the Austrian banknotes within their territories, thereby assuming responsibility for them. While the stamping proceeded, each State naturally closed its frontiers against the influx of Austrian crowns from other Succession States or from abroad. Smuggling therefore became at such times profitable business. Each stamping was accompanied by a boom in Austrian crowns in East Galicia proportionate to the advantage which smugglers could realise in the stamping of the banknotes. But not all banknotes suited their purpose; for reasons perfectly known to none but the experts in the trade, smooth, strong banknotes were required—they had to be like " tinplates." Still, at one juncture the illicit money-dealers, usually known as the " black exchange," began feverishly to search for some particular series of Austrian banknotes, paying for them high prices irrespective of their condition. The outside world never got to know exactly the particular trade secret behind this transaction, but it was rumoured that the particular series was accepted in the late Austrian territories now joined to Italy, and from East Galician villages, through underground channels, these particular notes seem to have found their way to Trieste and the Trentino.

But the Austrian crowns, the Russian roubles and the Polish marks, to say nothing of the short-lived Ukrainian hrivni, were all soon to recede before newcomers from the West—the American and Canadian dollars. During the period pre-

IN AN EAST GALICIAN VILLAGE

ceding the war hundreds of thousands of Jews and peasants from East Galicia had gone overseas, the Jews mainly to New York, the Ukrainian peasants to Western Canada. There is hardly a Jewish family in East Galicia which has no relatives in the United States, nor a village from which a few peasants at least have not gone to Canada. For years these emigrants had now been cut off from their homes, and the money remittances, which prior to 1914 used regularly to be sent by them to their relatives, had not been forthcoming. The money accumulated in the hands of the emigrants, and appreciated in a way which no one could have foreseen. Before the war the American dollar was worth about 5 Austrian crowns, early in 1920, 100 Polish marks, in the summer, 200, in the spring of 1921, almost 1000, in the autumn, about 6000 to 7000 marks. The returning emigrant, the unskilled labourer from Canada, the holder of some poor, hard-earned 1000 dollars, on his return home found himself a millionaire, a master in his own old village.

He had suffered much in Canada, and had worked and saved patiently; he had spent the best years of his life among strangers, despised and bullied, facing difficulties and situations which only his inexhaustible patience had enabled him to overcome. It was the thought of the eventual return to his own village which had kept up his courage. And now the return was more glorious than he could ever have expected. Others had fought in the war and suffered from its ravages, but he, the man from overseas, the *Kanadnik*, the *dolarnik*—owner of dollars—was the conqueror.

For this, however, he was neither loved nor admired nor welcomed. He, who during the many years among strangers had dreamed of the return home, was now looked upon by his own people as an undesirable stranger and an intruder. Each Government in turn which had sent the East Galician peasants into battle had promised them " homes fit for heroes," land to those who had shed their blood. The idea had struck deep roots in the mind of the East Galician peasant, who would claim land even from the Polish Government, say on the ground that he had fought in the Russian Bolshevik army. What does he understand of the quarrels between his various masters? All he knows is that he had been told to fight, and that he had fought; that he was promised land as reward, and that he is waiting for it to the present day. And while he waits, the *dolarnik*, who can afford to pay high prices, snatches it away from him. With bitter irony the East Galician peasant speaks of the " warrior from Canada," and the entire village presents a united front against the man who had been away while they suffered. Still, they finish by bowing to the omnipotent dollar. Foreign exchanges bring home to peasants in the remotest villages of East Galicia who it was that won the war and to whom the honour is due which is Cæsar's.

The dollar, American and Canadian, has become the standard currency of East Galicia. Land and houses are bought and sold in dollars alone, and the dollars themselves have become an important object of trade. On the market day in a small East Galician town the first hour or so is spent on inquiries concerning the exchanges of the day, and every peasant knows the relation of dollars to Polish marks and of the American to the Canadian dollar. There are, of course, local fluctuations, and arbitrage between neighbouring market towns is carried on by the Jewish traders. In every village there is some Jew who deals in exchanges, and the Jewish "brokers" from the nearest district town know of every *dolarnik* in the surrounding villages and how many dollars he possesses. If such a trader gets a tip from some bigger money market that the dollar is rising, he will race from one dollar-man to another and try to make the most of his prior knowledge. Still, by now the peasants themselves have become experts on foreign exchanges, well in touch with various "brokers," and take good care before they part with their treasure. But once the dollars have passed to the money-dealers they wander from the district town to Lemberg, from there to Cracow or Warsaw, then to Berlin, finally to return to the West in payment of German reparations or European debts.

About Christmas of last year [1921] a friend of mine, a big landowner from East Galicia, went on a trip to Italy, taking with him Canadian dollars. In December a clerk in a big Italian bank offered him the American rate for Canadian dollars—he did not know that there was a difference between the two currencies. In January a big Vienna bank offered much less for Canadian dollars than they were paid for in the world markets—they said they had never dealt in Canadian currency and had no market for it. But when at the end of January my friend returned to East Galicia—just about the time when the pound sterling and the Canadian dollar were appreciating against the American dollar—his Jewish village agent informed him that the Canadian and not the American dollar was now the thing to buy, and the rate between the two given to him by his agent closely corresponded to the exchange as quoted in New York, Montreal and London.

LORD FIFE AND HIS FACTOR [1]

("*The Spectator*," May 29th, 1926)

WILLIAM ROSE was factor and confidential friend to Lord Fife, and their correspondence, which lasted from 1763 till about 1800, together with accounts, bills, etc., all carefully preserved, filled "seven immense cases." Lord Fife knew its value and, in 1788, wrote to Rose:—

> "I wish some time, at leisure hours, you could arrange all my letters and libel (*sic*) them by the year, only just to separate them on business from general correspondence. I am certain I could make a pretty good history of many events, if ever I took time to review them, with the additional recollection of my mind—but this only speculation, for I never shall think of such a thing."

Nothing was done, and it was left to the present editors to "disentagle the valuable from the useless," read and sort some 20,000 letters, and choose from them for publication. Their workmanship points to the selection having been

[1] "Lord Fife and his Factor. Being the Correspondence of James, second Lord Fife, 1729–1809." Edited by Alistair and Henrietta Tayler.

made in a competent manner. Amateurs in history-writing are primarily people who take themselves more seriously than their subject, which certainly cannot be said about the authors of this book. They have done their work with care and devotion, and in an interesting series of well-annotated letters have given a vivid picture of one of those who formed the political set in Great Britain; this, as presented by them, makes a story, to some of us, at any rate, more interesting than any novel.

Lord Fife sat in the House of Commons from 1754 to 1790; till 1784 for Banffshire, which, between the Union and the first Reform Act, the Duffs represented for fifty years, and after 1832 without break from 1837 till 1893. He was no place-hunter; "I am in such a way in the world," he wrote to the Duke of Newcastle in 1754, "as to have little or no occasion to trouble your Grace with demands." But, though independent, he usually supported the King's Government, considering this the proper rule of Parliamentary conduct. Whig orators and historians have managed to confuse Tory gentlemen biassed in favour of authority with parasites intent on places and pensions, while the Tory accounts of the "Whig oligarchy" give an equally incomplete picture of the other side. A series of monographs about minor Members of Parliament, whose names and ideas are hardly ever considered and whose influence is usually underrated, would yield a different picture of one of the most gifted, active, inventive generations in British history, which, by its wit and love of humorous stories, has created an unduly derogatory legend about itself. The authors of this book have done the redeeming work for their own ancestor, simply by letting him speak for himself.

Lord Fife's political thinking at the time of the American Revolution is typical of a vast volume of British opinion. Though from the first anxious to avoid war (of which, as a true Scot, he disliked the expense), in January 1775 he could not join Chatham in " praising the *Loyal* Americans for all they had done, and desiring to move the King for the immediate recall of the troops from Boston." In 1776 he saw that " we gain no credit by our operations in America," and by 1777 wished for " a period to this American war. Our most sanguine and victorious expectations will not make all up, we are exhausting ourselves." In February 1778 he welcomed Lord North's Conciliatory Proposals as " the only means of getting out of the horrid scrape we are in," adding :—

> " I pray God that punishment may fall on the heads of those who have made so bad a use of the great exerted force of this

Country and misspent so much blood and treasure. . . ."

He voted (against the Ministers) for a special war-tax on Government salaries and pensions, and was becoming sarcastic about the King himself:—

> "The King is amusing himself with going about to visit ships, etc. . . . It looks like playing with rattles and whistles when so tremendous a power is armed to attack us. The Toulon fleet is certainly sailed . . . ours is waiting till great Personages be amus'd with the sight of it."

Still, he continued to support the Government, as is shown by the circular letter from Lord North in November 1779, inviting his attendance. But by 1783 Lord Fife had travelled the full length from North to Shelburne, whose Government he supported on the peace treaty in February 1783:—

> "I have no connection with them, but I love Peace and wish to give my vote of disapprobation of this, and abuse came but ill from a set of men who has brought the bad peace on us, for I think whatever is humiliating in it is owing to war-makers, and not to peace-makers."

In 1789, during the King's illness, Lord Fife's warm monarchist feelings once more became apparent; he did not, like many others, turn towards the expectant, jeering heir—his heart " unfeignedly " prayed for the King. After his recovery Lord Fife went to Kew, but when he saw the King mount his horse, " went to the other side of the road to see and not to be seen "; the King, however, hailed him, and addressed him in the most friendly manner :—

> " All this I bore and returned my grateful thanks. He then called out : ' Lord Fife, you are no gambler, you are no rat.' I then forgot all distance between King and subject, took him by the thigh, prayed the Almighty to bless him, and added : ' Yes, Sir, I am at present a gambler; my greatest stake is on that horse; for God sake take care of it, don't ride too hard.' "

Lord Fife's correspondence, of which politics form but a small part, admirably displays the cares, business and interests of a big Scottish laird in the latter part of the eighteenth century; also his mentality, unlike that of English lords or country squires, and completely different from that of the man about town which is most familiar to us from contemporary literature. Even his humour is different, composed of terse common sense and good temper, dry and unpolished, sometimes personal and even coarse. His mind was free of cant; on the death of a friend he writes to Rose :—

> "I think your wife expected a legacy, but I suppose he has forgot that, otherwise I should have heard more regret for him. Nothing on the death of a friend calls forth more affliction than a legacy."

Where other people might grow angry, Lord Fife remains humorous; thus after having suffered a loss of about £200 through a cousin of Rose's, he remarks :—

> "When you have done with such cousins as that, of your own, I can furnish you with some of mine, in the same stile."

But his humour does not spare people; on one occasion, describing things which he sends home from London, he mentions "one hen fully as large as your wife. I hope she shall be as breedy" (Mrs. Rose had twelve children). And Rose's own person invariably was in for it; thus in the letter of March 29th, 1777 : "I receiv'd your letter from Edinr., it was all over snuff nose-drops, so I condole with you on that accomplishment"—annotated on the back by William Rose: "Lord Fife anent snuff-taking. *Nota*. Gave it up on this reproach, 25th March."

But directly on this banter in Lord Fife's letter

follows a sentence which makes one's imagination wander to things unrecorded:—

> "There din'd here last Sunday *Genl. Grant*, Genl. Fraser, Col. Morris, Lord William Gordon, and Troup, so you see I am washing away offences in a moderate way."

As the editors add, " these were some of Lord Fife's political opponents"; but yet another interest attaches to their persons. " Genl. Grant" was probably Francis Grant of Dunphaile, M.P. for Elginshire from 1768 till 1774, when he was ousted by Lord Fife's brother, Arthur Duff; he had served in North America in the Seven Years' War, commanding the Royal Highland or 42nd Regiment.[1] " Genl. Fraser" was Simon Fraser, M.P. for Inverness-shire, the son of the Lord Lovat executed in 1747, himself attainted but pardoned; barred by Hardwicke from standing for Parliament in 1754, he proved his loyalty in the Seven Years' War by raising the Fraser Highlanders and serving with them under Wolfe;

---

[1] To begin with I thought that " Genl. Grant" was James Grant of Ballindalloch, M.P. for Wick Burghs, home on leave from America, where he had served in the Seven Years' War, been Governor of East Florida 1763–73, and was now serving once more; and where his over-bearing manners had done more harm than his service had done good. But on further consideration I am inclined to think that the " Genl. Grant" here mentioned was Francis Grant of Dunphaile.

and in 1776 he again raised two Highland battalions for service in America. " Col. Morris " was undoubtedly Staats Long Morris, M.P. for Elgin Burghs, a New-Yorker by birth, brother of the American revolutionary and ambassador, Gouverneur Morris; he married the widow of the third Duke of Gordon and died a general in the British Army. A dinner with these men in the year of Saratoga, at the height of the American crisis! But perhaps they did not talk about America at all; foremost in their minds was probably the old feud between the Duffs and the Gordons.

FAMILY HISTORY

(" *The Morning Post*," September 8th, 1926)

MOST family histories in this country are written by women. Country house fires destroy historical MSS.; many family histories do the same in a more elaborate though, fortunately, less final manner.

If their authors would but observe a few simple rules! A " Primer of First Aid " enjoins : " If there is time, call in a doctor." There is time, in history-writing—therefore start by consulting a specialist.

You undertake the work because you possess the materials; reproduce as much of them as you can and be sparing with your own contributions. Do not compile an elaborate " background " from elementary text-books. Lord Oxford and Asquith has suggested that standard versions, one Liberal and one Conservative, be written of the Home Rule crisis of 1886 for insertion in biographies of that time. Repetition would then at least be restful. But, still better, flatter your reader by crediting him with a knowledge of elementary facts, and discreetly refresh it in an incidental manner.

Stammer in speech produces irrelevant sounds; in writing, verbiage. Suppression of the superfluous is the essence of good writing. Do not attempt to cover embarrassment by becoming talkative, jocular or patronising; overcome it by work. The pleasant, non-committal smile which may suit tea-parties, changes into a nauseating grin when fixed in print.

Your chief task is properly to annotate your material; identify the people mentioned, ascertain whether any of your documents have been published before, and if so, whether the two versions agree, collate texts and accounts of events. Give references and do not omit dates.

It is not difficult to trace even the minor people in political correspondence. There is Marshall's "Genealogist's Guide," with references to genealogical works and to the most important local histories—the antiquaries of the eighteenth century did not suffer from inverted snobbery and knew that the history of the manor-houses was the political history of England; Musgrave's "Obituary"; the index of the *Gentleman's Magazine*, 1730–1817; Foster's and Venn's Registers of Oxford and Cambridge undergraduates, etc., etc. There are G.E.C.'s "Complete Peerage" and "Complete Baronetage"; Douglas-Paul for Scotland; the various works of Burke, in their many editions; Hunter's "Familiae Minorum

Gentium," etc.; and, for the lives of writers of doggerel, the "Dictionary of National Biography." Last but not least there are the catalogues in the British Museum, and in the Reading and Manuscript Rooms very kind supervisors ready to help and advise.

But in identifications remember that the sameness of name is not sufficient proof, especially in ages when initials were few and hyphenated names were rare: further evidence of identity is required. Exercise your common sense and keep alert.

One last hint: never state anyone's constituency and term in Parliament without having consulted the official "Return of Members of Parliament," published in 1878.

Neglect of this rule has made some of the best writers of family history commit egregious blunders.

THE END

Printed in Great Britain by
Richard Clay & Sons, Limited,
bungay, suffolk.

By L. B. *NAMIER*

2 vols.   8vo.   30s. net.

THE STRUCTURE OF POLITICS
AT THE
ACCESSION OF GEORGE III.

"Mr. Namier has written a book which will be indispensable to anyone who wishes to understand English domestic politics in the eighteenth century. It is a masterly piece of research into the system of Parliamentary management, a field which hitherto has been virtually unexplored."—*The Times.*

"Mr. Namier's . . . knowledge of almost every source, both printed and manuscript, in any way bearing on . . . eighteenth-century politics is so wide as to be almost uncanny. . . . Mr. Namier's investigations, contained in these two volumes, are far more exhaustive than anything of the kind hitherto attempted."

The Times Literary Supplement.

"This is the most important book on the politics of eighteenth-century England published since Lecky, and a more important book than that."

KEITH FEILING in *The Observer.*

SKYSCRAPERS

NAMIER'S STRUCTURE OF POLITICS
—*Press Opinions continued.*

"Mr. Namier's mass of interesting new material and his new views are a most valuable contribution to Georgian history."—EDWARD G. HAWKE in *The Daily Telegraph*.

"Mr. Namier . . . has managed to destroy more legends and modify more preconceived ideas than any historian of this generation. . . . The reading and digesting of these two volumes is the first duty of every serious student of modern English political history."
The Oxford Magazine.

"No student of our domestic history in the eighteenth century can possibly afford to neglect this work; and it is hoped that it will find a wide circle of readers."
D. A. W. in *The Cambridge Review*.

"No book that I know gives one so deep an insight into the politics of England in the eighteenth century as this."—LEONARD WOOLF in *The Nation and Athenæum*.

"An extremely interesting and important book."
The Daily Mail.

MACMILLAN AND CO., LTD., LONDON

By L. B. *NAMIER*

8vo. 25*s*. net.

ENGLAND IN THE AGE OF THE AMERICAN REVOLUTION

BOOK I. GOVERNMENT AND PARLIAMENT UNDER THE DUKE OF NEWCASTLE.

"The present volume makes an addition to our knowledge of the eighteenth century every whit as important as its predecessor, 'The Structure of Politics,' and has other merits of its own. . . . The general form of this work is as flawless as can be."

KEITH FEILING in *The Observer*.

"There is a touch of something unique in Mr. Namier, a new method of tasting the intellectual pleasures of history. There are so many different ways in which things happen, or can be truly described as happening. Gibbon's is one, Carlyle's another, Macaulay's a third. Each is true, yet taken by itself each is false, for no one of them is the whole truth. In Mr. Namier's narrative things 'happen' in yet another way—the Namier way. And it is one of the truths . . . Mr. Namier is a new factor in the historical world."—PROFESSOR G. M. TREVELYAN in *The Nation and Athenæum*.

"Another volume from the deadly hand is . . . an event in historiography, and all the learning, all the mastery of technique, and more than the previous allowance of humour, are again displayed for our admiration."—*The Oxford Magazine*.

"NAMIER'S ENGLAND IN THE AGE OF THE AMERICAN REVOLUTION"
—*Press Opinions continued.*

"The chief attraction of the book will be found in his masterly descriptions of most of the characters that appear prominently in the political proceedings of these three years: the King himself, Bute, Newcastle, Pitt, Count Viry, as well as of some of the less prominent personalities, such as Dodington, George Grenville, Hardwicke and his sons, Lincoln and the budding Charles Townshend."—*The Times.*

"He is nothing if not a serious historian, and the reader thirsting for a sensation is more than likely to be given a table of percentages. There is scientific method and deep purpose behind his work, and his profound knowledge, meticulous care, acute critical powers and philosophic bent of mind are used in the service of real scholarship. His method is virtually a new approach to the study of the eighteenth century."

The Week-End Review.

"No student of the period can possibly afford to neglect this important contribution to knowledge; and if he is conscientious he will be obliged to consider the necessity of revising his previous conclusions. . . . An extremely scholarly and valuable work."—D. A. W. in *The Cambridge Review.*

"His style is marked by lucidity and the poise of the historian who is more interested in the truth than in shadowy rationalizing. He has made a contribution of distinct importance to the knowledge of the Revolution's background in England."—*New York Times.*

MACMILLAN AND CO., LTD., LONDON